<u>G O D</u>

a
n
d

<u>Ronald Reagan</u>

God moves in the affairs of men

By

Harry von Bulow

This book is a work of non-fiction. Names and places have been changed to protect the privacy of all individuals. The events and situations are true.

© 2003 by Harry von Bulow. All rights reserved.

No part of this book may be reproduced, stored in a retrieval system, or transmitted by any means, electronic, mechanical, photocopying, recording, or otherwise, without written permission from the author.

ISBN: 1-4107-8644-7 (e-book)
ISBN: 1-4107-8645-5 (Paperback)

This book is printed on acid free paper.

1stBooks – rev. 11/18/03

GOD and Ronald Reagan
God moves in the affairs of men

CHAPTER I

A man from Dixon, Illinois changed the world!

He was the world's modern David. Instead of slewing the giant Goliath, he tamed the Russian Bear. For fifty years communist Russia had been the country's archenemy. It had intimidated the world with its military might; its atomic capability and space vehicles. It had put democracy and capitalism in retreat. The Soviets seemed to be the favorite model for the world. Krushev boasted that Russia would bury the west. Some form of socialism, communism, or Marxism reigned in the Third World Countries. In the 1970's the Soviet nuclear arsenal passed that of the U.S. Between 1974 and 1980 nine countries fell into the Soviet orbit. And in 1979 Russia invaded Afghanistan.

The man from Dixon changed all this:

AND WITHOUT FIRING A SHOT!

On June 12, 1987 he went to the Brandenburg Gate at the Berlin Wall; a Wall that had split Germany in half; a Wall that had imprisoned over seventeen million people; a

Harry von Bulow

Wall that caused the bloody death of one hundred and fifty three attempted escapees. And on that summer day, standing before that stark, gray wall, he spoke six words which shook the world: "MR. GORBACHEV, TEAR DOWN THIS WALL!"

And the Wall came tumbling down like the Walls of Jericho.

AND IT CAME DOWN WITHOUT THE SOUND OF A RIFLE SHOT!

The man from Dixon, of course, was Ronald Wilson Reagan.

Henry Kissinger termed it: "The greatest diplomatic feat of the modern era."

When Reagan became president the country needed a heart transplant. The old, pioneering spirit that was the true spirit of America seemed atrophied. The country was standing still and everything seemed to be falling apart. Inflation was in double digits: eighteen to twenty two percent. There was an energy crisis. Gas had been thirty-five cents in 1970, now it was a dollar and a half. Senator Kennedy advocated gas rationing. Unemployment and poverty rates were high. A verbal fungus had invaded congress: It didn't know what to do. The military also had its problems. Nothing seemed to work. When they tried to free the hostages in Iran everything went wrong. They landed in the wrong place – a sand pile in the desert. The blowing sand jammed their helicopter's engines and they had to scrub the mission and return home. And eight men died.

The hostages were still in Iran when Reagan was inaugurated.

But two hours later they were free!

On their way home!

AND IT ALL HAPPENED WITHOUT FIRING A SHOT!

GOD and Ronald Reagan
God moves in the affairs of men

Was it a miracle? Was his mother Nelle right, that God would lead her son; that good would ultimately conquer evil?

Reagan was like the prophets of old, the ancient ones that filled the Old Testament: Isaiah, Daniel, and Ezekiel.

AND LIKE THEIR PHOPHECIES, HIS PROPHECIES ALSO CAME TRUE

On his watch the world changed:

Dictatorships collapsed in Chile, Haiti and Panama. And nine more countries moved toward democracy:

Bolivia	(1982)
Honduras	(1982)
Argentina	(1983)
Grenada	(1983)
El Salvador	(1984)
Uruguay	(1984)
Brazil	(1985)
Guatemala	(1985)
Philippines	(1986)

Fewer than one third of the countries in Latin America were democratic in 1981; more than 80% of the region was democratic by 1989.

On Reagan's second term free elections were held in Nicaragua. Apartheid ended in South Africa. In 1987 the Soviet Union agreed to dismantle and destroy its SS-20 missiles. A year later Moscow pulled its troops out of Afghanistan. Poland held free elections and Lech Walesa became president. Suddenly all of Eastern and Central Europe was free.

These events didn't happen by chance. The leader, the architect of the change, was Reagan, a man of God, and a true believer. He was the prime mover.

Harry von Bulow

Lou Cannon, who wrote three books on Reagan said, "I regard Reagan as a puzzle. I am still trying to understand the man." Historian Edmund Morris, Reagan's official biographer, considered Reagan the most incomprehensible figure he has ever encountered. Donald Regan, Reagan's Chief of Staff said he couldn't figure out his boss at all.

There is a phrase from the Bible, "The Lord confounds the wise." And it probably refers to a man like Reagan, who was deeply religious.

Here was a man, who had the most important job in the world, yet seemed relaxed, even casual the way he went about it. He was always friendly, gregarious and seldom ever raised his voice.

While the "wiseman of the world", couldn't understand him, the American voter found him to be the leader they were looking for. They elected him and reelected him by stunning margins of victory. He was a man like Lincoln, who the people felt was honest and a man they could trust. Both were outdoor men, physically strong and tough. And absolutely fearless!

Again: Who was this man named Ronald Wilson Reagan?

Who was this man from the tiny town of Dixon, Illinois?

Was he someone anointed by God; like Jacob, or David, or Moses?

GOD and Ronald Reagan
God moves in the affairs of men

CHAPTER II

Luke Chapter 2:39-41 "And the child grew and waxed strong in spirit, filled with wisdom and the grace of God was upon him."

It happened early in the morning, about five o'clock. Nelle turned over in bed and tapped Jack, her husband on his shoulder.

"Better call the doctor."

Jack blinked, rubbed his eyes, and glanced at the clock. "Are you sure?" he mumbled.

"Yes, I'm sure," said Nelle.

Then Jack struggled out of bed. And then went to the living room and called the doctor.

A moment later he returned to the bedroom and Nelle. "He's on his way," said Jack.

"Better heat some water."

Jack went to the kitchen. Filled the teakettle and put it on the stove.

Harry von Bulow

The doctor arrived about twenty minutes later. As he entered the small apartment he turned to Jack. "Why can't they have their babies in the daytime?" And then, "Where is she?"

And Jack led him into the bedroom.

* * * * * *

About three hours later Ronald Wilson Reagan entered this world. A swift smack on his bottom and a tiny scream announced his coming. He was a healthy, big baby, weighing over ten pounds and he had all his toes and ten fingers, a good straight nose and two blue eyes. Nelle checked every part of him as she held him in her arms. Then she held him up to Jack.

Jack studied the tiny nude body, then shouted, "It's a boy!"

"Yes," said the doctor. "He's a boy." And then turning to Nelle, "Better rest, dear." And he tapped her gently on the shoulder.

She nodded sleepily.

The doctor smiled at Jack and then left.

Jack kissed his wife on the forehead, gently pinched the tiny toes of his new son.

"I'll be back later," he said and headed out to celebrate.

* * * * * *

He ended up at his favorite bar, the Tampico Saloon among his old cronies and bar regulars. It was a dark and dingy place: sunlight never penetrated its walls. The smell of stale beer permeated the place. The old walnut bar was soaked with it. There was a rail where you could rest your

GOD and Ronald Reagan
God moves in the affairs of men

foot on and shiny, golden spittoons for those who chewed tobacco.

As he entered he shouted, "Drinks on the house!" And then holding up a goblet of beer he proudly announced, "It's a boy!"

And his friends cheered.

"Named Ronald Wilson Reagan!"

And they lifted up their steins of beer and cheered. "Here's to Ronald Wilson Reagan. Jack's new heir!"

"Sounds like an English nobleman."

"It's Irish, man!" an angry retort.

"Through and through."

"From top to bottom."

"A to Z."

"Here's to the Irish gentleman, Ronald Wilson Reagan!"

"From top to bottom."

"A to Z."

"Another drunk, slightly slurred, "May he live a long and noble life!" And then hiccupped. "From top to bottom. And then he started unzipping his pants. "I gotta go to the can."

For the next three days Jack disappeared: He was on a drunk celebrating the birth of his son. Jack Reagan is an Irishman, who loves his booze.

He is Tampico's town drunk.

* * * * * *

Ronald Wilson Reagan was born on February 6, 1911 in a little apartment above the bank building in Tampico, Illinois. The Reagans were poor; times were tough. His father Jack Reagan never found it hard getting a job, but he had trouble keeping one. He was a shoe salesman, who liked his Irish Whiskey.

Harry von Bulow

The marriage itself between Jack and Nelle was a strange one. Jack was Catholic; Nelle was Protestant. Jack was an alcoholic; Nelle was a devoted Christian. One of her favorite sayings was: "The Lord will provide." And during their stormy marriage she depended more and more on the Lord to pay the rent and feed the children. But they survived together, mainly because Nelle had the faith and patience of Job.

His mother wasted no time in introducing Christ to her children. As soon as Ronnie was weaned, she sat him on her lap, opened the beautiful picture book of Jesus and began his Christian education.

As she slowly turned the pages of the book, the wonderful story of Jesus of Nazareth unfolded. And little Ronnie, with eyes wide open, was completely enthralled. Some times his pudgy tiny fingers would touch the colored picture and he would laugh and look up at his mother and she would smile and then point to the saviour and say very slowly, "Gee-zus. Gee-zus."

And baby Ronnie would try to imitate the sounds, only it usually came out more like" "Ma-ma...Ma-ma."

And she would smile and kiss him on the cheek and repeat the word: "Gee—zus...Gee—zus."

And as the days and weeks passed, Jack asked Nelle when she was going to have the boy baptized.

"Not for awhile," she replied.

It surprised Jack. "Neil was baptized when he was a baby." Neil was their first child and he was almost three now.

"I know."

"Why not Ronnie?"

"I want him to know what it means." And she paused a moment. "Like Jacob and Esau." And then she said, "He is the younger one. The blessed one."

"So what!" And Jack shrugged his shoulders.

GOD and Ronald Reagan
God moves in the affairs of men

"He'll decide when he's ready to be baptized." And she emphasized the pronoun "he". "I'm leaving it up to him."

Jack didn't pursue the subject any further. He knew that when his wife made up her mind, there was no changing it.

* * * * * *

And then in the evening, when the shadows lengthened, and the lights were dimmed, Nelle would take her two little boys to the small corner bedroom. And they would put on their pajamas and brush their teeth and they would kneel down beside their bed and Nelle would kneel beside them and she would lead them in prayer. At first it was the most simple one:

> "Now I lay me down to sleep,
> I pray the Lord my soul to keep.
> If I should die before I wake,
> I pray the Lord my soul to take."

And then later, she taught them the Lord's Prayer: "Our Father, who art in heaven, etc." And she put a picture of the Lord on the wall of their room.

But, best of all, she told them wonderful stories;stories about Daniel and the Lion's Den; and David and Goliath, and Moses and Jonah and the whale and Noah and the Great Flood and lots more. She read them aloud, out of the Bible and she made them all come to life. She made them real, breathing people; real roaring lions and tigers. She dramatized them all with the skill of a born storyteller. Her Noah's Ark was especially great. She could do a whole repertory of animal sounds: The chattering monkeys, the parrots talking among themselves, elephant's

Harry von Bulow

honking, the plaintive cry of a wolf, the growl of a big brown bear. And Ronnie and Neil hung on to every word, every sound she made.

And as she turned down the night-light in the little room, she would always end her stories with some beautiful final line:

"Boys, everyone has a special part to play in this world, God's world."

And the two little boys would nod, not really understanding.

"There is a divine plan for all of us." And then she would quote Romans 8:28. "...all things work together for good to them that love God."

And then they closed their eyes and she would smile and the boys would fall asleep.

Mothers are the heart of a family. And certainly Nelle was the heart of the Reagan family. She kept the family together. She gave it its moral and ethical foundation. And her textbook was the Holy Bible. Nelle not only believed the scriptures, but she herself led a Holy life. And Ronnie took after his mother.

Nelle was the Good Samaritan of Tampico. Some people even considered her a saint, for she visited patients in the sanitariums and mental hospitals and brought cookies and Bibles to incarcerated prisoners. After the men were released, she often took them into her house until they found a job.

Nelle never saw anything evil in another human being and she was an incredible optimist and so was her son. Reagan once said, "We were poor, but I never knew it."

Nelle would tell her boys that everything happens for a reason. They may not understand the reason at the time, but eventually they would.

And her son Ronnie imaged his mother.

10

GOD and Ronald Reagan
God moves in the affairs of men

* * * * * *

At the age of four young Reagan could recite all sixty-six books of the Bible. Nelle called it God's gift. In essence, he had a photographic memory. Nelle discovered it when she had the two boys memorize the books of the Bible. Neil had considerable trouble: it took him over a week to learn them. Ronnie read them once and could recite them, word for word, verbatim within an hour after reading them.

At the age of five young Reagan taught himself to read. He followed his mother's fingers as they moved under the words of a story, usually a Bible story.

One day his father came home and found his son sitting on the floor, reading the newspaper.

"What are you doing?" asked his father.

"Reading," said Ronnie.

"Oh yeah?" He didn't believe him. "Then read me something."

And Ronnie did.

It so shocked his father that he went running out of the house, shouting, "My son can read! My son can read!"

* * * * * *

Young Reagan was all boy. He could have been Mark Twain's Tom Sawyer, or Huckleberry Finn. He was like a brand new battery, fully charged, fully energized. He seemed to be in perpetual motion; always moving; always on the run. And, in the summertime his energy seemed to be multiplied by the sun as if its warm rays added a nuclear bolt to his already mega-powered system.

He loved to swim and, on hot days, he and Neil and their friends headed to the canal for a dip. They stripped,

Harry von Bulow

tossing their clothes off in a pile in the grass, stretching their nude, young bodies in the warm sun. It made them feel good, vital; made them feel strong and invulnerable. And then young Reagan, the leader of the band, would take a deep breath and dive into the cool, brown water. A moment later his head bobbed up out of the water, his hair pasted to his head with muddy water dripping over his face.

"C'mon in!" he shouted, "the water's fine!"

And Neil and their friends would join him.

And sometimes they'd do the great chute-de-chutes off the side of the cement incline. It was coated with algae and slippery as ice. It made a great sliding board. And sometimes they stood up and skated down its sides, or used their bottoms as a sled, or even their stomachs when they wanted to hit the water head-on, their faces taking the full blast of the water.

Then there was strawberry-pickin' time and making five cents a box. Two boxes equaled one movie at the Tampico Opera House, where Tom Mix and his horse Tony were playing; or maybe it was Hoot Gibson; or maybe some African serial with snakes and voodoo men. Those strawberries introduced you to a whole new world, a world that excited your curiosity and imagination. Ronnie loved the movies. And, I suppose he must have dreamed of one day being in them himself; of saving the girl with the long golden curls and riding off into the sunset with her.

Sometimes they wandered over to the Tampico Stockyards; climbed the fences and gates and chased the cows, or played tag with the pigs and sows. And intermittently they would stumble or fall and their pants and feet would be smeared with cow manure, or perfumed with sow dung. And with that distinctive aroma they'd come bounding home and as they hit the front door Nelle would know exactly where they had been.

"In the stockyards again!"

GOD and Ronald Reagan
God moves in the affairs of men

Ronnie bowed his head guiltily.

Neil rubbed his hands nervously.

"Go upstairs," commanded Nelle. "Take all your clothes off and get in the tub!"

Neil moaned. "Do we have to take a bath?"

"Yes," confirmed Nelle. "C'mon. Let's go!" And she meant it this time.

Ronnie began undressing as he headed for the bathroom. He tossed a shirt on the chair, sox on the floor and wiggled out of his short pants.

"And give me your dirty clothes," shouted Nelle.

Sometimes in the evening, maybe on a Saturday night, Nelle would boil weenies and they would pile mustard and ketchup and onions on them and they would sit on the front porch and eat their hot dogs and drink their cokes and watch the sun go down.

To Ronald Reagan summer always seemed to go faster than any other part of the year, as if God made the days shorter; maybe eighteen hours instead of the regular twenty four.

And, of course, you couldn't go swimmin' in the wintertime.

In September young Reagan made his debut in the First Grade of the Willard Elementary School in Tampico. It was a successful opening: His grades were superb; straight "E's" for excellent.

But while young Ronald was enjoying his first academic success, his father was being fired by the Fashion Shoe Emporium. They said he was spending too much time at the local tavern. And, although Jack was a pleasant man and quite handsome, no one in their right mind would hire him in Tampico. So, he sought a new venue. Some place where he was unknown, a total stranger. He picked Monmouth, Illinois.

Harry von Bulow

It wasn't long before Jack got a new job in Monmouth selling shoes. His Irish smile and handsome features appealed to the older women in this fair city. And, of course, the family found a new home in Monmouth. And young Reagan found a new school. It was the Central Elementary School of Monmouth. He was registered in Second Grade, but was quickly moved to the Third Grade. "He's too smart for the Second Grade," said the principal. So young Reagan skipped a grade.

That same year an epidemic of "Spanish Flue" invaded Monmouth. Ronnie and Neill seemed to be alright and Jack's alcoholic addiction acted as its own immunity system, but Nelle, God's child, became critically ill. In fact, the doctor told Jack that his wife was dying.

"And I don't know what else I can do for her," he said and he put his stethoscope back into his black leather bag.

Jack ushered him to the door.

"I'm sorry," he said.

Ronnie went into his mother's bedroom and kneeled down beside her bed and prayed.

His mother lay still and silent, her eyes were closed. She seemed to be asleep.

Reagan's father headed for the kitchen. He went to the icebox and took out an old, moldy, rotting piece of cheese. It had turned green. He cut it into small slices and put it on a plate and took it into Nelle's bedroom. Ronnie looked up as his father entered the room. He didn't understand what he was doing.

Jack woke up Nelle and then lifted her up into a sitting position and held out the plate. He took a piece of the moldy cheese and pushed it into her mouth.

"Eat it," he said.

She moved her mouth; made an ugly face, then swallowed it.

GOD and Ronald Reagan
God moves in the affairs of men

He gave her more and without a sound, only an ugly look on her face, she ate it. And then another piece, and another.

And the children prayed.

Jack sat up with her the rest of the night. Young Reagan found his father early the next morning holding his mother in his arms. And her eyes were open. She spoke to him in a soft, quiet voice. And Ronnie and Neil sat beside her on the bed and she smiled.

And the days passed and Nelle grew strong and one morning Ronnie woke up and he could hear a familiar sound: It was his mother doing the family washing.

His mother was well.

Was it the moldy cheese (a source like penicillin) or was it the prayers that saved her? He didn't know for sure.

* * * * * *

Then in the fall it was back to Tampico. His old boss Pitney rehired Jack. And just to make sure the Reagan family would have a place to live, he let them use the apartment above the store free of charge.

The leaves turned golden and red and burnt orange and then flew away in the cold winter wind, their colors floating in the sky as if bidding goodbye to a beautiful autumn. Then there was Halloween and black goblins and black witches with pointed black hats and faces with long, crooked noses and all kinds of scary things and Ronnie and Neil scavengered the neighborhood for candy and cookies and other goodies. And they came home with chocolate on their faces and jellybeans in their hands and a stomach gorged with candy. They had never had it so good. The night had been a resounding success. Nelle only hoped they wouldn't be sick the next day.

Harry von Bulow

Flakes of snow fluttered down on Tampico in early November. The temperature plummeted to five below zero. And men and boys got out their snow shovels and cleared the sidewalks and driveways. And cars skidded around corners and kids pulled their knitted caps down over their ears and put on warm mittens and heavy coats and jackets. And Ronnie and Neil put on their long underwear and black sox and wool knickers and galoshes.

* * * * * *

It was November 11th. It had been snowing most of the afternoon, but that didn't stop Tampico from having an Armistice Day Parade. It went right down the main street and everyone, who had an American Flag, waved it proudly.

At school the children constructed a handsome snowman with a red, white and blue top hat and in his arm he carried a beautiful American Flag. They had borrowed the flag from the handyman at the school.

It was almost four in the afternoon, when Ronnie started home. It was still snowing hard, but young Reagan didn't mind. He loved the snow. It covered the dark places, the dirty corners, the old houses, the muddy cars, the slushy streets and turned the black arms of the trees into white crosses.

He cut across Seventh Street and then started sliding and running and sliding (he could get home faster that way) toward his house in the middle of the block. As he reached the front yard he hesitated a moment, then came to an abrupt stop. There was a large, dark lump of something resting or laying in the front yard. It did not move. It was like a small hill and almost completely covered by the snow. He approached it cautiously. It could be the neighbor's big shepherd dog. Then it began to move a little. As young Reagan drew nearer, it became obvious to

GOD and Ronald Reagan
God moves in the affairs of men

him that this strange mound was actually alive and after further investigation realized that it was a man lying in the snow. He put his hand out and carefully brushed the snow away from the man's face.

The man smiled and said, "Hi."

It was his father!

"The war is over!" exclaimed his father.

He is drunk. And he had gotten sick and vomited all over his coat.

"I'll give you a hand, dad," said Ronald.

His father smiled. Although somewhat pale, he seemed jovial and quite happy. The snow had apparently not frozen his good cheer. It was obvious that the Irish Whiskey had kept his spirits warm.

"The war's over, Ronnie," he repeated.

Ronald nodded. "Yes, I know." He paused. "It's been over for two years." And then he said, "I'll help you get up, dad."

But he found it almost impossible for him to pull his father up. He was too big and heavy for young Ronnie. So, finally Jack helped solve the problem: He first got on his knees and then rising from there and holding on to his son's shoulders he reached an upright position. And then resting his arm around his son's shoulders they struggled into the house.

Ronnie led his father to his bedroom, took off his coat and shoes and put him in bed.

As Jack plopped down on the bed he shouted, "The war's over!" Then waved to Ronnie and fell sound to sleep.

* * * * * *

That night, just before going to bed, Nelle took young Reagan and Neil aside and she explained their

Harry von Bulow

father's "medical" condition. "He has a sickness," she said. "We must be patient with him."

Ronnie nodded.

Neil nodded.

"A sickness," repeated Nelle. And then she and the two young boys kneeled down and said their prayers.

But even with handsome Jack back on the job, tenderly tending to the toes of middle-aged women and softly massaging their dainty ankles, the Fashion Boot Shop of Tampico seemed destined for bankruptcy. So Pitney courageously made a dramatic, and bold decision.

"We must move to a bigger, more lucrative market," said Pitney. "We will move the Fashion Boot Shop to Dixon."

Dixon, Illinois was a thriving town of over six thousand people. And it was not too far from Tampico. In fact, Pitney felt that he and Jack could move the entire stock of the Fashion Boot Shop themselves to the new location. So, one bright spring day they loaded up Pitney Bowles' old model "T" with all the shoes and headed for Dixon, where Pitney had rented a new store right downtown on the main street of Dixon, Illinois.

Once again the Reagan family packed up their belongings and headed for another town.

"I feel like a gypsy." She told Jack one night. "It's time we settled down and stayed in one place for awhile."

Jack agreed, although he seemed less concerned than Nelle.

"It's hard on the children."

Jack nodded.

"I just get acquainted at church," she continued, "and we move." She paused and studied his face. It hadn't changed a bit. "And the children have been in three different schools in four years. It's not healthy. They need a sense of belonging and security." Jack nodded.

GOD and Ronald Reagan
God moves in the affairs of men

"They can't get it moving from one place to another."

* * * * * *

But in Dixon Nelle found a nice, old square house that she loved. It was on South Hennepin Avenue. It was two story; had three bedrooms and a large living room with a stone fireplace. And a nice big yard for the children to play in. This was really a step-up from their tiny apartment over the shoe store in Tampico. She hoped and prayed that this lovely house would be her home for a long time.

The year was 1920.

* * * * * *

Another day, another school. That Fall young Reagan entered the fourth grade at Dixon Elementary. Changing schools didn't seem to bother him. He made new friends easily. He is quite tall for his age and a good athlete and won a prize for throwing the football the longest distance. The teachers liked him because he was a good student with good manners. He received excellent grades.

Public speaking was his forte even at this early age. On Parent-Teacher's Day, he along with two other students, were chosen to recite their favorite stories. It was a special honor only accorded to the best students of the Fourth Grade class. Mary Jane Cole, a shy, but rather beautiful, little redhead was the first to perform. She chose "The Cat and The Mouse." Then Carl Smith read an Aesop Fable entitled: "The Boy Who Cried Wolf." The final one on the program was young Reagan. He recited from memory "The Sermon On The Mount." Holding his mother's Bible in hands his voice rang out clear and confident throughout the Assembly Hall.

Harry von Bulow

"And seeing the multitudes, he went up into a mountain; and when he was set, his disciples came unto him.

And he opened his mouth and taught them, saying:

Blessed are the poor in spirit; for theirs is the Kingdom of Heaven.

Blessed are they that mourn; for they shall be comforted.

Blessed are the meek; for they shall inherit the earth.

Blessed are they that hunger and thirst after righteousness; for they shall be filled.

Blessed are the merciful; for they shall obtain mercy.

Blessed are the pure in heart; for they shall see God.

Blessed are the peacemakers; for they shall be called the children of God.

Blessed are they, which are persecuted for righteousness' sake; for theirs is the kingdom of Heaven.

Ye are the salt of the earth, but if the salt has lost its savor, wherewith shall it be salted? It is henceforth good for nothing, but to be cast out and to be trodden under foot of men.

Ye are the light of the world. A city that is set on a hill cannot be hid.

Let your light so shine before men, that they may see your good works, and glorify your Father which is in heaven."

Young Reagan closed the Bible and walked quietly back to his desk in the class. And, for a seemingly long time there was a lucid stillness, an almost oppressive silence. No one spoke. Everything stopped. And then the teacher said, "Thank you Ronald."

GOD and Ronald Reagan
God moves in the affairs of men

Later, after the program, the teacher took young Reagan's mother aside, and with a gentle smile on her face said, "I think he should be an evangelist."

That same year his mother and he gave a recitation at the Church of Christ. And early in May he made his dramatic debut with a monologue entitled: "About Mother."

When he was twelve he told his mother that he wanted to be baptized. "I want to declare my faith and be baptized." So, on June 21, 1922 Ronald Wilson Reagan was baptized by the minister of the First Christian Church and was fully immersed in the Hennepin Canal.

And when Jesus was twelve, the family journeyed to Jerusalem for the Feast of the Passover, but when they started back they couldn't find their son, and for three days they frantically searched for him. They finally found him in the Temple, standing among the Scribes and Pharisees, who were greatly impressed with his knowledge. But Mary and Joseph were not pleased with his behavior and in an almost angry tone, they asked, "Where have you been?" And Jesus replied, "I must be about my father's business."

When young Reagan was fifteen he led Dixon's Annual Sunrise Prayer Meeting at the Disciples of Christ Church. Dressed in his Sunday best he stood in the middle of the Hennepin Avenue Bridge and with head bowed, eyes closed, he led the crowd of worshippers in a sunrise prayer. Everyone wore jackets and coats on that Easter Sunday. It was a chilly forty-eight degrees, but the sun was bright and the sky a deep blue.

At 9:30 A.M. young Reagan had a Sunday School class to teach. Then at 10:45 there was the main church service with a final Holy Communion service.

* * * * * *

Harry von Bulow

Summer vacation was swiftly approaching. It was early in May when young Reagan went down to the Southside YMCA in Dixon and signed up for a lifesaving course. Two weeks later he was certified by the Red Cross. In the meantime, he had heard of a job opening at Lowell Park along the Rock River. Mr. Graybill, the manager, was looking for a lifeguard for the summer. He immediately headed for the Park. Young Reagan had won the cross-river swim the year before so Mr. Graybill knew him pretty well and knew he was qualified.

"You've got the job," said Graybill. "It pays fifteen dollars a month and all you can eat at the lunch stand."

* * * * * *

There is a certain magnificence about being a lifeguard at fifteen years of age. First, you get a better tan than anyone else. You sit in this elevated chair and survey and direct the action below you. This creates a certain regal feeling. And, if you are tall – about six feet, and good looking with nice legs and broad shoulders and a trace of hair on your chest, you can lead a rather pleasant social existence. And young Reagan possessed all these qualities, plus one: He was a conscientious lifeguard, who took his job seriously.

* * * * * *

I suppose a person always remembers the first time; your first date, your first kiss, your first love. Reagan remembered his first rescue.

The Rock River can be an angry river at times and a dangerous one. It is not like swimming in a pool. It has a current, an independent way of life. It can be angry and rough and sometimes smooth as silk. Its ways can fool an

GOD and Ronald Reagan
God moves in the affairs of men

inexperienced swimmer. And sometimes when the devil is in the waves it can drown even a good swimmer.

This was Reagan's first rescue. She was twelve years old. Her name was Elizabeth Conn and she had gone out too far. The current was too swift, too strong for her little arms. And, when he heard her choking scream, he dove in, swam furiously toward her, catching her just before she went down for the third time. And then finally, he had brought her back to safety.

He would never forget her name: Conn. And he thanked the Lord that she was alright. And Elizabeth would never forget him.[1]

* * * * * *

But that night, lying in his bed, just before going to sleep, he noticed a little cloud hanging over his head. It was like a little, furry ball, about a foot or so in diameter floating on the ceiling above his head. At first he thought he might have something in his eyes. He blinked once, rubbed his eyes, and then glanced up. It was still there. It must be a shadow from some light, he thought, although it was apparent that there was no light in his room. He closed his eyes. I will forget about it. I'm sure it is nothing, he thought. And he fell asleep.

But the next night it was there again: The same little, furry cloud, about the size of a basketball hovering above his head on the ceiling. He blinked. Rubbed his eyes. Looked again. And it was still there. He studied the room. Nothing had changed. He looked for a light. There was no light. And wherever he looked the little cloud

---

[1] Years later, when he became president she wrote him a beautiful letter congratulating him on his victory and again thanking him for saving her life.

Harry von Bulow

followed his gaze. Finally completely fatigued, he fell asleep.

But the next morning he asked Nelle, his mother, about it.

She wasn't sure. "There was no light on in the room?" she asked.

"No, I'm sure of that. I checked it." Then he paused. "Mother, do you believe in a Guardian Angel?"

"Possibly." She wasn't sure.

"And the Holy Spirit?"

"Absolutely! The Holy Spirit is with every believer!" she said. "It is part of the Trinity."

Young Reagan nodded. He was well acquainted with the Trinity; the Father, Son and Holy Spirit. He had heard his mother tell about it many, many years before.

The next night he looked for the little cloud again on the ceiling of his room. He closed his eyes; then opened them again. But it was gone.

* * * * * *

At seventeen he described his optimistic outlook in a poem published in the Dixon High School Yearbook.

"I wonder what it's all about, and why
We suffer so, when little things go wrong?
We make our life a struggle,
When life should be a song."

And life was like a song for Reagan at Dixon High. He was on the football team, president of the senior class, an officer in the school dramatic society and that year he won the Annual Cross-Country Swimming Award.

Life at this time was a song.

GOD and Ronald Reagan
God moves in the affairs of men

The spring rains came early that year, greening the countryside: the weeds in the nearby fields next to Jack Reagan's place began to grow with new life and vigor. Even their front yard, once dead brown with Bermuda grass began to green-up. Even the Rock River, once frozen over with ice, started showing new life, roaring with new gusto down its channel. The old buildings downtown took on a shinier glow, even the famous Dixon Arch looked like new. It was obvious spring was here.

In the last of May 1928 there was the Dixon High School graduation. Ronald Wilson Reagan was one of those lucky ones to get a diploma. The graduating class did not wear caps-and-gowns. Few families had money to spend on renting a cap and gown. Most of the graduates came in their Sunday-best, a few wore bib-overalls, some of the girls were in gingham dresses, a few in flour sacks, but they all looked bright and happy and shiny clean.

Nelle and Jack watched as Ronald received his diploma from the high school principal. It was a joyous occasion.

* * * * * *

In June he was back at his regular summer job as lifeguard at Lowell Park. He loved the summer; the warm sun and everything seemed alive and glowing. And then there was the future, his future: college, football (he loved football) and girls and dances. Everything about it was exciting. He was anxious to be on his way! And Nelle was all in favor of college. "It's important that you get your degree," she said. "It will help you the rest of your life."

And young Reagan agreed with her completely. He immediately applied for entrance to Eureka, a small college in DeKalb, Illinois. It was not too far from his hometown of Dixon and not too expensive. But he knew, he would

Harry von Bulow

have to save every penny that he made at Lowell Park for him to have sufficient funds to pay his tuition, books, etc. at Eureka, but that challenge didn't seem to bother him.

* * * * * *

It was August 8, 1928, almost 9:30 P.M. and Mr. Graybill had just closed the bathhouse and had turned off all the lights in the park. He and young Reagan were about to leave. There was no moonlight and hardly a star had ventured out in the darkness. Reagan glanced at the swirling black river.

Then there was a cry in the darkness. It came from the river. It startled both men.

Young Reagan looked at Graybill.

Both stopped. "Did you hear something?"

"Yes."

Then there was a second cry.

Young Reagan tossed off his glasses, raced toward the river and plunged into the dark, swirling water. He swam furiously toward the sound. He saw nothing. Every thing was black; like swimming in the bottom of a well; only there was a swift current. He felt it pushing against his body. It carried him in a curve away from the sound and he had to fight his way back to where he thought he heard the cry. He paused and listened a moment. Nothing. Silence. Where is the voice? He began slowly swimming again; guessing where the sound had come from. He listened for a splash. A cry. Some sound he could follow. There was only the memory of a sound coming from somewhere; a sound no longer audible. An arm rose from the dark water and grabbed him around the neck. It surprised Reagan for a moment. It was a man's arm. Strong. Muscular. The man was choking him. Reagan took a deep breath and slid under water. The deeper he went the looser the arm got around

GOD and Ronald Reagan
God moves in the affairs of men

his neck. Finally the man let go and frantically struggled for air above the water. Reagan came up at his back. Put his arm around him. The man fought for a moment. Then collapsed. The man was dead weight now. And Reagan started swimming upstream against the current of the river. Finally, almost completely exhausted, Reagan got back to Lowell Park. Mr. Graybill helped him pull the man out of the water. And Reagan applied artificial respiration and he was revived. His name was James Raider.

The next day on August 3, 1928 the Dixon Evening Telegraph ran an eighteen-point banner headline:

"PULLED FROM THE JAWS OF DEATH"

It was the story of Ronald Reagan's heroic rescue of James Raider.

* * * * * *

In 1929 the Great Depression had just begun. Thirty-two percent of the U.S. working class were unemployed. Herbert Hoover was president. Jack Reagan's Fashion Boot Shoppe had gone broke: it's doors shuttered. The Reagans were in tough financial straits. There was no unemployment compensation; little or no Federal relief and Jack Reagan would never accept any kind of government dole anyway. Neil had gone to work at the local cement factory. Ronnie was still at Lowell Park and Nelle had become a seamstress.

The only folks with money were the bootleggers. The eighteenth amendment had ignited this new industry: selling illegal schnapps. And Al Capone ruled the roost. He had turned Chicago into a bootlegger's paradise. He owned the mayor, the city council and almost every cop on the beat. Some of his power had even leaked into the little town of Dixon, Illinois. And Jack Reagan was more than

Harry von Bulow

happy: He had found a solution to his "Sickness" as Nelle called it.

In the Fall young Reagan attended Eureka College. After paying his tuition he had thirty-five dollars left. He immediately began an intensive search for a job; a night janitor's job appeared as a good possibility.

In January his father was hired by the Red Wing Shoe Company at the magnificent salary of two hundred and thirty dollars a month. He mentions to Nelle that he'll be on the road a lot. "There's a bit of traveling to it," he explained. But she's happy he's employed once again.

Jack doesn't seem to mind the traveling either: The seeing of new faces, creating new friends, enjoying some of the social amenities of a traveling salesman. After all, Jack's handsome. He's tall, masculine looking and a genuine Irishman, who loves most everyone – including blondes and brunettes.

And speaking of romance, Ronnie starts dating the preacher's daughter, Margaret Cleaver. She's a neat little thing, who lives at the parsonage. She's active like Ronnie in drama and sports. They make a good pair.

* * * * * *

When he was a junior at Eureka College, Reagan finally made the varsity. He played right guard for the Eureka Red Devils, but he was far from being a star: He had bad eyes – could hardly see out of one (it was 20/2000) and was slow and a little clumsy, but he had a wonderful, wild and indomitable spirit.

In the Illinois Wesleyan game in 1931 Reagan played across the line from a monster name Tony Blazine. He was a Hall of Famer and an All American. Blazine weighed in at two hundred and fifty pounds and was tough as nails. Reagan hit the scales at one hundred and seventy.

GOD and Ronald Reagan
God moves in the affairs of men

As to be expected Reagan spent most of the game flat on his back. But he survived and he was still on his feet when the final whistle blew.

It is true that Reagan prayed before every game; sometimes aloud, sometimes silently. It is also true that on that day, when he was going to face Illinois Wesleyan and All American Tony Blazine, his prayer was longer, protracted and more specific. For on that fateful day, intermittently, you could hear a prayer or two rising up out of the grassy playing field. It was brief, but most dramatic: such as "Save me O'Lord! Save me!"

* * * * * *

The following week the Eureka Red Devils football team was on a road trip to Elmhurst, Illinois to play the Elmhurst Tigers, a league rival, but the old bus was a little late chugging into Elmhurst. It was early in the evening when they finally arrived at the La Salle Hotel.

The Eureka football team, tired and hungry, was just about ready to disembark from the old bus, when the manager of the hotel glanced into the bus.

"Hold it a minute." And then he raised his voice. "Just a minute fellows!"

All action, all movement stopped.

The Manager of the Hotel LaSalle motioned to the coach. "Could I see you for a minute."

"I'm right here," said Mac.

"I mean privately," said the manager and he spoke in a whisper.

"Sure," said Mac. "What's the trouble?"

And the Manager drew Mac aside and they went into the lobby of the hotel. Reagan followed them.

29

Harry von Bulow

Inside the Manager whispered, "The hotel doesn't take gentlemen of color." He paused, a little reluctant to continue. "You got two of them."

"What!" Mac's voice caromed throughout the little hotel lobby.

"I'm sorry."

"You mean to tell me you won't let Burghardt and Jim Rattan sleep in this joint!" And his voice rattled the rafters.

The Manager nodded.

"Hell! We'll all sleep in the bus if we have to." And Mac was ready to storm out of the hotel lobby, when Reagan grabbed him by the arm.

Mac stopped. Looked at Reagan. "Yeh?"

"You know Dixon isn't far away," whispered Reagan. "I'll take the two of them home with me. No problem."

"Are you sure your parents won't mind."

"I'm sure," said Reagan. "But I'll need some cab fare."

The coach pulled out his wallet. "How much do you think you'll need?"

"Gimme ten," said Reagan, "and I'll bring you back the change."

The coach smiled. "Make sure you do. That's about all I got to buy breakfast for these guys."

A few minutes later the Elite Cab Company arrived at the hotel. Reagan, Burghardt and Jim Rattan piled in and headed for the Reagan home in Dixon.

His mother Nelle was surprised to see Reagan and his two black friends, but she greeted them with a cheerful smile. "There's an extra room at the top of the stairs. Has only one bed, so you'll have to share."

Burghardt and Rattan nodded, and hopped up the stairway.

GOD and Ronald Reagan
God moves in the affairs of men

Alone with his mother, he said, "The hotel was full."

Nelle grinned. "Don't try to fool your old mother."

Reagan was about to reply, when she interrupted him.

"They're Negroes," she said. "They're black," and then she quoted the Bible. "There's no room at the Inn."

Reagan nodded, then kissed his mother on the cheek and gave her a loving hug. "Goodnight," he said.

"Sleep tight," she rhymed.

* * * * * *

On April 10, 1930 the Northwestern Drama Department's Fifth Annual Tournament was underway and the Eureka Players were scheduled to do Edna St. Millay's "Aria de Capo". Reagan had the role of Thyrsis, a shepherd boy.

As a result of his performance Reagan was named one of the six best actors in the Annual Drama Tournament. Even Professor Garret Leverton, Director of Northwestern's School of Speech was impressed. He took Reagan aside.

"You should make acting your career," he said.

"Thank you."

"You have a natural talent."

Reagan smiled and thanked him again.

And then they announced the top six actors of the Drama Tournament.

"And number three is Ronald Wilson Reagan of Eureka College."

Enos Cole, a Eureka football star, patted Reagan on the back. "Time for Hollywood!" And he laughed.

Margaret Cleaver, another thespian and Reagan's girlfriend kissed him sweetly on the cheek.

Harry von Bulow

* * * * * *

1930 was a busy year for Reagan at college. He was on the varsity football team; was editor of the Eureka Yearbook; elected to the College Senate and was acting president of the Booster's Club. In his spare time he gave swimming lessons.

But financially he was in trouble. In fact, in his senior year at Eureka he was $37.00 in the red. His life savings came to $455.00; his expenses: $492.00. These figures were carefully noted in his accounting book. Realizing he was faced with a deficit in his last year, he went to the president of the college and explained his situation.

"I think this can be taken care of," said the president and he promptly made him a small loan of $115.00. This more than covered his deficit. And thus Reagan graduated from Eureka $162.00 in debt. But Reagan was never in favor of deficit financing, and after he was employed by Radio Station WHO in Des Moines, he immediately liquidated this obligation.

* * * * * *

That following summer on July 25, 1931 Reagan again made the headlines on the front page of the Dixon Evening Telegraph. He had just made his fiftieth rescue at Lowell Park.

A few months later, a clock was placed along the Rock River at Lowell Park, bearing a simple message: "From 77 grateful people." They were the 77 whose lives were saved by Ronald Reagan.

GOD and Ronald Reagan
God moves in the affairs of men

CHAPTER III

Now armed with his degree from Eureka College and overflowing with confidence, young Reagan, age twenty-two, borrowed his dad's old Oldsmobile and headed for his first job interview. It was in Davenport, Iowa, a two hundred and fifty watt radio station with the call letters: WOC. It was owned by the Palmer Chiropractic Corporation.

An old, bent-over, angry man named Pete MacArthur ran the station. "What the hell do you do?" he asked Reagan.

"I'm a sports announcer," said Reagan.

"What experience do you have?"

Reagan paused a moment.

"Well…!" demanded MacArthur.

"None," said Reagan.

"You have a lot of guts wasting my time!" he shouted.

Reagan was not going to be intimidated by this old man. He remembered the battle he had with the All

Harry von Bulow

American football star Tony Blazine and this guy was little, and old and bent out of shape.

"I played a lot of football," he said. "I played for Eureka College and I know the game."

"But can you announce it, describe it?"

"Absolutely." Reagan was confident.

"Ok, go in the studio. We'll see what you can do." And he led Reagan into this rather simple room, where a mike hung from a boom. "This is it now, Reegan."

"It's Reagan," corrected Reagan.

"Ok Reagan," said MacArthur. "It's all yours."

There was a rather long pause.

"Well, I'm waiting," MacArthur seemed irritated.

Then Reagan began. He remembered the Eureka game with Elmhurst. He picked the final quarter. The game was tied. Eureka had the ball. It was on the forty-yard line. He described the movements of the quarterback. The wide receivers, the shifting from the "T" formation into the box and the quarterback barking out the signals and then the ball came back to the quarterback and he handed it off to Simmons, and Simmons headed around right end, his blockers ahead of him. He was at the thirty yard line, then the twenty, ten and a touchdown."

He looked at the station owner.

"Not bad," he said. "We'll try you out," And then he said, "You'll get ten dollars a game."

He didn't stay long at WOC, Davenport, Iowa. The regular sportscaster returned a few weeks later, and Reagan was dismissed. But, in the meantime, he had become acquainted with Joe Maland, manager of WHO in Des Moines and he hired him. This was a good break for Reagan for soon WHO Radio would go to 50,000 watts, enough power to cover almost all of the U.S.A. and give him national prominence.

GOD and Ronald Reagan
God moves in the affairs of men

The first question Maland asked Reagan when he arrived in Des Moines was: "Can you do track?"

"Sure." Reagan had never broadcast a track meet in his life.

"The Drake Relays are coming up next month," said Maland. "Do you think you can do them?"

"Absolutely," said Reagan. "No problem."

At that time the Drake Relays and Penn Relays were two of the greatest track events in the country. Only the fastest, world-class runners attended one or the other. And every track enthusiast compared the records and times between the two meets. Were the Penn Relays better than the Drake Relays? Or vice versa. Actually it varied from year to year, but it was a major event every year.

Reagan broadcast the Drake Relays like a veteran, and Maland was more than pleased. He increased his salary by ten bucks and made him Sports Director of WHO. He would do all the major sports events at the station.

At radio station WHO in Des Moines Reagan became one of the best play-by-play announcers in the country. His forte: always describing the game in the present tense: as it was happening; not in the past tense as most radio announcers did.

And he had a wonderful creative mind; a dramatic flare that made the game come alive. Even when he was taking it off the telegraphic tape, he dramatized it in such a way that made it sound even better than it was. Many listeners preferred listening to Reagan's telegraphic reports than those originating at Wrigley Field, the home of the Chicago Cubs.

At the zenith of his broadcast career he was picked as one of the six best sports announcers in the country.

But besides sports Reagan loved horses. There was always a little cowboy in him. He loved to ride. And, as luck would have it, there was a cavalry post at Ft. Des

Harry von Bulow

Moines. They had experts to teach you to ride and Reagan liked to excel in everything he did. So, he went out to Ft. Des Moines and applied for Officer's Training. It was there he learned to ride in the precise, U.S. Calvary style. He would however, never forget his final examination.

It was in the spring and the trees were just budding and the birds were singing, but on that day, it was pouring down rain, and a cold wind was whipping down from Canada. On his drive to the Fort that morning he thought they would certainly postpone the final. For he could hardly see driving to the Fort, the heavy rain was almost blinding, and although his windshield wipers were working vigorously, he could hardly see the pavement, or cars ahead.

When he reached Fort Des Moines, he noticed a number of the cadets were dressed in their rain gear. He immediately went to the Adjutant's Office and reported in.

The Captain glanced up from his desk.

"It's sure wet out," said Reagan.

The Captain nodded, and then, "You're Reagan?"

"Yessir."

"Got your raingear?"

"Yessir."

"Your final will be in an hour."

Reagan never forgot that final ride for his commission. It was a wild, especially dangerous ride, under the present conditions, riding his stallion leaping over six foot barriers, the horse's hoofs slipping and sliding in the wet, muddy turf. But this is the army, he thought. Rain, snow or sleet the war must go on. And he closed his eyes and flew over the high barriers as the rain splashed in his face.

And he became a second Lt. In the reserve.

* * * * * *

GOD and Ronald Reagan
God moves in the affairs of men

At WHO Reagan felt he was really in the money. He was making a hundred dollars a month; more than he had ever made before, and doing what he loved to do.

The Lord has been good to me, he thought.

Reagan had always tithed. His mother Nelle had taught her children to always give a tenth to the church. "This is God's planet. You're breathing His air and feasting on His land. You owe Him at least a tenth."

So, Reagan always gave a tenth to the church, but there was something else bothering him at this time. His brother Neil was attending Eureka College. And it was Depression Time.

Reagan went to his pastor in Des Moines. "I have always tithed to the church," he said, "but I am faced with a problem. My brother Neil is going to Eureka College. He has little, or no money. The ten dollars I give the church would be a great help for him."

The minister quietly assessed the anguish on his face.

"I wonder if it would be alright if I gave the ten dollars to my brother Neil, instead of the church. He certainly needs it. But I don't want to slight God."

The minister smiled. "I don't think God would hold that against you."

"I'll try to make it up another way," said Reagan.

"I'm sure you will," said the minister.

Harry von Bulow

CHAPTER IV

And Jesus told the story of the Good Samaritan: "A certain man went down from Jerusalem to Jericho and fell among thieves, which stripped him of his raiment and wounded him, leaving him half-dead.

But a certain Samaritan, when he saw him, had compassion for him. And went to him and bound up his wounds and brought him to the Inn and took care of him."

* * * * * *

It was a warm Sunday evening in Des Moines. Sultry defines it better. Iowa heat is always packed with moisture. Reagan opened the bedroom window, hoping to get a little fresh air. It was almost eleven o'clock. He had just put on his pajamas and had crawled into bed when he heard a raucous outside his window. An angry, snarling voice was shouting at a woman. Reagan jumped out of bed.

GOD and Ronald Reagan
God moves in the affairs of men

Looked out his window and down below a man was holding up a young woman.

And she was screaming. "Take everything I've got, but let me go!"

Reagan grabbed his forty-five revolver and in the glow of the street lamp outside he could see the woman. She was a nurse from nearby Broadlawns General Hospital. Her hands were in the air; the robber was stopping to pick up the woman's purse, when a deep, commanding voice echoed in the street below.

"Leave her alone!" shouted Reagan. "Or I'll shoot you right between the shoulders!"

The man glanced up and seeing a large, black forty-five revolver pointing in his direction, fled the scene.

Standing in his pajamas Reagan shouted out the window to the young girl. "Wait for me! I'll be down in a minute!" Reagan grabbed a robe, put on his slippers, peered out the window again. "Just hang on!" he shouted.

And the poor girl standing in the dark, still shaking with fear, waited for Reagan to come down to the street.

A moment later he arrived. "You from Broadlawns?"

She nodded, still too shaky to talk.

"I'll escort you back to the hospital," he said. And he put his arm around her. "You'll be ok," he tried to comfort her. "You'll be fine."

She nodded but still couldn't speak. She was still so frightened. Finally they reached Broadlawns General Hospital. He took her to the door.

Her voice finally came back. "I'll never forget you," she said. "I don't know what I'd done without you."

He shook her hand. "You'll be alright."

But she held on to his hand an extra moment; a minute or two and she sputtered, "Thank you. Thank you. God bless you." And then went into the hospital.

Harry von Bulow

* * * * * *

Early that spring he talked to Joe Maland, Manager of Radio Station WHO, about sending him to the Cub's training camp at Catalina, California.

"I could do a lot of personal interviews with the players. Get to know them. Give me a little richer background of them. Make the broadcasts more authentic."

Maland liked the idea. "We'll try it," he said.

And soon Reagan was riding the Northwestern streamliner west. It was his first trip west and it opened up a whole new world to him. He saw for the first time the magnificence of the country; the rolling, green hills of Iowa, then on the flat lands of Kansas and Nebraska – you could see for miles and then up the grade (two engines now) to the Rockies, snow-capped and majestic. The top of the world. And then down the slopes into the tunnels, into the darkness, then the light and reaching the desert floor; hot, burning, cactus and nothing except a hot wind and then San Bernardino; palm trees, people in shorts, the window warm and finally Los Angeles.

As he stepped off the train a gentle, warm wind caressed his face, ruffled his hair slightly. He took a deep breath. Gazed around the L.A. Station. Smiled. I like this, he thought. Three days before he was wearing a heavy trench coat and being blown across Grand Avenue in Des Moines. He hailed a cab. "To the Biltmore," he said, just like John Wayne might have said it, or Cary Grant, or Gig Young.

The next day he took the big white steamer to Catalina. When he arrived he immediately called Charley Grimm, manager of the Cubs, and told him of his mission.

"Great!" said Grimm. He was happy to get any extra publicity he could for the team. "Our bus leaves the

GOD and Ronald Reagan
God moves in the affairs of men

hotel every morning about eight. Be there and you can ride out with the team to the practice field."

This was a great break for Reagan. And, from then on he rode on the player's bus. What a treat! Guys he had never met, but talked about on the radio became sort of his friends.

The first day he sat next to Gabby Hartnett, the Cub's great catcher; and then there was Hack Wilson, the home run hitter and Kiki Cuyler and Jurges at short, and Stan Hack and Charley Root and Guy Bush. He loved the moment and his broadcasts that followed had all the fun and excitement his fans loved to hear. Maland was glad he had given him the go-ahead for the idea. It seemed to perk up the station and the Hooper Ratings soared.

But even good things have to come to an end, and the Cub training camp ended a week before the season opened. Reagan took the big white steamer back to the mainland and checked into the Biltmore again. There was something else on his mind.

* * * * * *

The next day he took a bus to Republic Productions where a "WHO" band happened to be playing. Its manager got him admitted to the studio and introduced him to a casting director. Later, he did a read for the director.

That night he went to the Biltmore Bowl. He sent a note backstage to Joy Hodges, who was performing there. He had known her before in Des Moines. They had a drink together after her show.

"I have visions of becoming an actor," he said. "I'd like to get a screen test."

"I'll see what I can do," she said. And then looking at him: He was wearing heavy horn rimmed glasses. "Just don't wear those glasses ever again!"

Harry von Bulow

George Ward, Joy Hodges' agent arranged an audition with Max Arnow, the casting director of Warner Brothers, the following day at the Burbank Studios.

Arnow's first words were, "Are those your own shoulders?"

Reagan nodded.

"Let me hear your voice."

Reagan spoke.

"Is that YOUR voice?"

"It's the only one I have."

Arnow handed him a script. "Memorize it," he said. "We'll shoot a test on Monday."

Reagan arrived an hour early for the test. The makeup man studied his hair. "You always part it in the middle?"

Reagan nodded. "Yes."

"We're changing it."

"Oh."

Little more was said and the screen test seemed very brief; sort of anti-climactic. The Director made no comment, except, "Thank you."

And Reagan left. The next day he boarded the Golden State Limited and headed back to Des Moines. He was back at work on Friday, April 2, when a telegram from George Ward arrived. It stated: "WARNER BROS OFFER CONTRACT STOP SEVEN YEARS STOP ONE YEAR OPTIONS STOP STARTING AT $200 A WEEK."

This was the beginning of Ronald Wilson Reagan's film career.

GOD and Ronald Reagan
God moves in the affairs of men

CHAPTER V

Jane Wyman was born Sarah Jane Mayfield at St. Joseph's Missouri on January 1917. Her parents, not wanting a child, left their daughter with Mr. and Mrs. Fulks, a middle-aged couple, who were neighbors of the Mayfields. Jane was just five years old at the time. The Fulks, realizing the Mayfield's were never going to return to pick up their little baby girl, named her Jane Fulks. Mr. Fulks died in 1928 and Mrs. Fulks and Jane moved to the west coast. Jane Fulks attended L.A. High School and, when she was sixteen, married a young salesman named Ernest Wyman. The marriage lasted two years. Meanwhile Jane was singing and dancing her way in Hollywood musicals; finally getting a contract from Warner Brothers on May 6, 1936. About this time she met a man named Myra T. Futterman and married him after five martinis and a whirlwind courtship. He had a new Lincoln convertible, a spacious home in Beverly Hills, a Falstaff figure and a large

43

Harry von Bulow

bank account. He was thirty years older than Jane and could have been her father.

Reagan met Jane Wyman on the set of "Brother Rat" in July of 1938. It was a time when Hollywood was the Sodom and Gomorrah of the west; the sensual city: The ever present sunshine, mild air, fruits and flowers perfumed the entire atmosphere.

It was a world of sex. While Errol Flynn and Clark Cable screwed every young beauty in sight, Reagan kept his privates in his pants: Nelle's teachings seemed to haunt his mind.

"Brother Rat" was Reagan's and Jane's first real success. Jane was still married to Futterman. Reagan, although attracted to her knew she was married and he refused to pursue her in any romantic way.

Jane ultimately got a divorce from Futterman and then with her hormones blazing she concentrated all her female charm on Reagan, finally capturing him in a dramatic hospital scene.

Jane was supposed to have tried to commit suicide if Reagan wouldn't marry her. Hearing this Reagan rushed to the hospital and shouted, "I'll marry you!" as they were pumping out her stomach.

After about an hour Reagan left the bedside of his future bride, and with spirits soaring he headed for his mother and dad's place on Phyllis Avenue. He wanted them to be the first to know. And when he arrived he also found Neil there. Good, he thought. The whole family's here.

His first words were: "I'm going to get married!"

For a moment the family was stunned. No one said a word.

Finally Nelle said, "Good. It's about time."

"And what's her name?" asked Jack.

"Jane," said Reagan. "Jane Wyman."

GOD and Ronald Reagan
God moves in the affairs of men

"Have I ever met her?" asked his mother.

"I don't think so," continued Reagan. "She was in Brother Rat with me."

"Oh," said Nelle. And then, "Is she a Christian, Ronald?"

He wasn't sure. "I think so."

"What church does she go to?"

"I'm not sure, mother."

His father entered the conversation. "Is she Catholic?"

"I'm quite sure she's not Catholic," said Reagan.

His father continued, "I once knew a Catholic girl from San Diego who had fifteen children."

"Fifteen!" exploded Ronnie.

"You're spoofin' us," said Nelle.

"No," said Jack. "It is true. They had seven boys and eight girls."

Nelle shook her head.

"Now I remember," said Neil and then turning to his brother, "She was in Brother Rat."

"That's where I met her," said Reagan.

Neil sighed. "She is a beauty!"

Reagan smiled.

"Do you love her?" asked his mother.

Her son nodded. "Yes, mother I love her."

Then Reagan got up from his chair, went over to his mother and kissed her on the cheek. "I hate to say this, but I've got to go. I told her I'd be back tonight."

"She still in the hospital?"

"Yes," said Reagan. "She'll probably be released tomorrow," Then he headed for the door. As he opened it, he turned and waved and smiled, "Goodnight."

As the door closed the conversations ended. The room became silent. No one spoke for a couple of minutes.

Harry von Bulow

Each of them had their own thoughts roaming through their minds.

Finally Neil said, "What do you think?"

Jack responded. "She's a beauty! He can really pick 'em." Then he laughed. "Takes after his old man."

No one laughed.

Then Neil continued, "You know she's been married before."

This was news to everyone, and Nelle stopped rocking in her rocking chair and listened carefully.

"She was just a kid when she married Wyman."

"A kid?" asked Jack.

"Sixteen," said Neil. "About sixteen I think. She was in high school."

Nelle leaned back in her rocking chair and began to rock slowly back and forth.

"He was a salesman."

"A shoe salesman?" asked Jack.

"I don't think so." He paused a moment, then continued. "Something in advertising, I think." Another moment, then, "but I'm not sure. But she divorced him two years later."

"And...?" Jack was following every word.

"And then she met a man named Futterman. He was three times her age, but apparently had a lot dough."

"And...?"

"And she married him."

Nelle's rocking chair was moving faster now.

"And she recently got a divorce from him."

And then the room became very quiet, only the sound of Nelle's old rocking chair could be heard. It was moving rather quickly now.

Then Jack said, "How old is she?"

"Nineteen," said Neil.

GOD and Ronald Reagan
God moves in the affairs of men

"She's been a busy little girl," said Jack. "Two marriages and now a third and just nineteen years old. She oughta set a record by the time she's forty."

Nelle stopped rocking in her rockin' chair and then stood up and said, "I think it's time for me to go to bed."

Neil went over and kissed her.

"Maybe the third time is the charm," commented Jack.

And then as Nelle headed for her bedroom Jack called, "I'll be in in a little while."

Although Nelle never criticized Jane; never said anything derogatory about her; and always treated her with kindness and respect, in her heart she was dubious about the marriage's success. Jane was pure Hollywood; Reagan was pure Dixon, Illinois. Nelle wanted Ronald to marry a Christian girl, someone like the beautiful Rachel (Jacob's wife), or Isaac's Rebecca; someone who would make a good home for her son and their future children.

Jane was none of the above. Her whole life, her whole physical and psychological makeup was tied to the movie industry. She loved Hollywood; loved being an actress – and she was very good at it.

So, Nelle kept her thoughts to herself. Instead she quietly prayed that it would work out alright.

* * * * * *

Jack Reagan, Ronnie's father, died in 1941. Reagan was in New York at the time.

Nelle called him and told him of his father's death. "But don't get on a plane," she pleaded, "because if something happened to you I couldn't take it."

Ronnie returned by train and Nelle delayed the funeral until he arrived.

Harry von Bulow

That night something really strange happened to Reagan. While he was sitting in the chapel, feeling depressed and lonely, a voice – his father's voice, seemed to be saying to him, "I'm okay. I'm happy. Don't worry about me. I'm doing fine."

Reagan never spoke to anyone about this until many years later, when he was in his second term as president. He told Nancy about it. She thought, Lord how I would have loved that to happen to me, when my parents died. She envied him that peace of mind.

GOD and Ronald Reagan
God moves in the affairs of men

CHAPTER VI

Being a Lieutenant in the Reserve, Reagan was called up in '42, soon after the Japanese bombing of Pearl Harbor, but his eyes were so bad they were afraid to let him shoot a gun.

"How'd you get in the army?" asked the drill Sergeant.

Reagan shrugged his shoulders and smiled.

"I wouldn't trust you with a squirt gun!"

"Don't worry," said Reagan, "just point me in the right direction."

But they didn't let him fire a gun; instead they assigned him to a film-making group.

"He's an actor," said the Colonel. "Put him in the Hollywood Group."

And this group was comprised of some of Hollywood's most famous actors, including Errol Flynn, James Cagney, Marlene Dietrich, and Clark Cable. It produced most of the training films for Armed Services and created some of the most memorable and popular war films

Harry von Bulow

of the era. Among them was "God and Country", in which Reagan played a Catholic Chaplin. It was a perfect role for him: There was that missionary aspect to it and Nelle loved it. Next came "This is the Army", another winner at the box office; then "International Squadron" and "Knute Rockne, All American" in which he played George Gip, "Win one for the Gipper" became a popular phrase even when Reagan was running for Governor California. Next he was chosen by the army to narrate a secret, classified series called Project 152.

All in all, Reagan was happy and making all kinds of money. In fact, he was Warner Brothers' highest paid actor, making over one hundred and fifty thousand a year with a seven-year contract. He was just thirty-two years old and at the zenith of his movie career.

But a few things still bothered him.

* * * * * *

Discrimination was always a sensitive word with Reagan. In fact, he almost got into a fight at a party in Hollywood one night when a stranger made some anti-Semitic remarks.

And then a few weeks later he talked to Captain Bill Orr, a friend of his in the Service. "Do you belong to the Lakeside Country Club?"

"You know I do." It seemed a silly question to Bill. "So do you."

"Ever see any Jews there?"

"I dunno, why?"

"It's restricted," said Reagan.

"Restricted? How?"

"No Jews," said Reagan. I don't like that. "We should give up our memberships."

GOD and Ronald Reagan
God moves in the affairs of men

"Now wait a minute!" Bill was disturbed. "My mother and sister love the Place."

"I'm resigning," announced Reagan. And he not only resigned from the Lakeside Country Club, but then joined the Hillcrest Club, the favored location of Beverly Hills Jews.

Harry von Bulow

CHAPTER VII

Reagan joined the Screen Actors Guild in 1938. In 1947 he was elected their president. The SAG recognized his leadership qualities and he was reelected four times.

Charlton Heston said, "He was one of the toughest and shrewdest bargainers the guild had ever produced."

In the course of his tenure he dealt with some of the toughest movie bosses that Hollywood ever produced. Most of them thought Reagan was just a sweet, gullible guy, but in their reverie he seduced them, obtaining most everything he wanted. In the finale it was not Reagan's naiveté, but their own naiveté that made them capitulate. Reagan's gentleness, his good-natured style would always be a part of the Reagan mystique.

As president of the Screen Actor's Guild, Reagan would get his first sampling of the communist's technique. The Reds wanted to take over Hollywood and the motion picture industry. This would give them a fabulous avenue to promote their own communist philosophy.

GOD and Ronald Reagan
God moves in the affairs of men

The Reds wanted first to take over the motion picture unions. They knew that if they controlled the unions they would control the industry.

And they were not gentle in exercising their intentions. As one communist enforcer explained it: "One of the first ones we decided to take over was the scene painter's union. Some of these Hollywood queers didn't like the idea. So, I broke a few arms. I broke their painting arms. And the bastards stopped painting. Two guys would hold the painter and I would take his arm and break it over my knee. It worked out pretty dam good."

It was this kind of violence that was occurring on the movie lots. Every motion picture union craft was in jeopardy. Some of the producers and actors wanted to compromise with the Reds, but Reagan said, "Absolutely not!" And he started cleaning them out.

It wasn't easy. Many had infiltrated the writers, and actors unions along with motion picture crafts. The picket lines became violent and military. The state militia, at one time, was called in. And Reagan was advised to carry a gun for his own protection. There were vile and intimidating telephone calls to his home.

Reagan was called to Washington to appear before the House Un-American Activities Committee (HUAC). He did cooperate with the committee, but accused McCarthy of painting everyone, who disagreed with him, as a communist.

But Reagan's obsession with Union politics destroyed his marriage with Jane Wyman. They had been married for eight years. She hated politics and hated even more her husband being involved in it. But there was another key factor: Jane's career was just beginning to blossom. She was in the "Lost Weekend" and then the "Yearling". Two great movies, two major hits. And while she was learning her lines and trying to discuss a character

Harry von Bulow

portrayal, he was talking about the communists and how they were trying to infiltrate Hollywood.

In all it was too much for Jane: She filed for a divorce. She said he was boring. "I'm so bored with him, I'll either kill him, or kill myself."

It was shattering for Reagan. Divorce he had never considered. The Bible says, "For better, or worse." He could not understand her feelings.

One evening, deeply depressed, he got in his car and drove by Jane's house. He almost wanted to go in and beg her to take him back, but he kept on going. He headed down Hollywood Boulevard, passed the CBS studios and NBC, the flashing signs almost blinding his eyes. Then over to Phyllis Avenue, where his mother lived. He stopped the car in front of the house, and for a long time, he just sat and looked straight ahead, his mind wandering through a maize of thoughts. Finally he decided to go in. It was still early, about eight o'clock, but sometimes his mother would go to bed early. He rang the doorbell. A few moments later his mother answered the door.

She looked at him and smiled. "C'mon in, son."

"I was just driving around," he said. "And all at once, I'm on Phyllis Avenue. So, I thought I would see how you're doing mom."

"That's sweet of you, son."

They sat in the small living room, and she waited for him to begin the conversation. She knew he had come for a reason. She knew what he was going through. She knew it was the divorce. And it was killing him. But she waited for him to begin.

Finally he said, "It's Jane." He hesitated. "You know she's asked for divorce."

Nelle nodded. It had been in all the papers. You'd have to be blind, deaf and dumb not to have read or heard about it.

GOD and Ronald Reagan
God moves in the affairs of men

He began telling her how he felt; how he missed her. And that he had failed her. Divorce was hard for him to accept. "I could have done more," he said. "Been more helpful, or..." and his voice wandered off and then fell silent.

She listened sympathetically and compassionately. She knew what he was going through. She waited for him to continue, but he sat silent, just staring at her. Then she responded with words he had heard many years before. "Dear", she said and there was a soft consoling warmth in her voice, "remember everything happens for a reason. You may not understand it now, but eventually you will."

He looked at her and smiled. The words were like an old familiar song. He remembered them from long ago, as a child growing up, Nelle had always told them (he and Neil) that everything happens for a reason. "God makes it that way. And wait and see, it will be for the best." And she touched his hand and smiled. "You'll see."

He stood up, smiled and kissed her on the cheek. "Take care of yourself, dear," and he left.

* * * * * *

In 1952 he met Nancy Davis. She was having trouble with a communist black list issued by the House Un-American Activities Committee. There was some other actress with the same name as hers, who apparently was associated with the communists. Mervyn LeRoy suggested she meet with Reagan, then President of SAG, the Screen Actor's Guild. She called him and explained her predicament. They had dinner that evening at LaRue's and from then on they became a Hollywood item. They were married that same year and Bill Holden, a good friend of Reagan's, was his best man.

Harry von Bulow

Nelle was pleased with her son's choice. Nancy was different. True, she was an actress, but preferred being a wife first. While Jane Wyman's life was centered on her own career, Nancy's was centered on Ronnie's. She gave up her acting career and began making a home for him. Her goal was to make him happy, give him children and, above all, give him all her attention and love. She became sort of the counterpoint in his life, creating a wonderful balance that gave his life a sense of completeness and fullness that he had never known before.

But there was a period in the fifties when things began to change for Reagan. He no longer was the shining star of Warner Brothers. Younger men like Zachary Scott and Robert Hutton were getting the key roles now. And, while Reagan was sitting on the sidelines, Gig Young and Wayne Morris landed a post war movie. In order to pay the bills Reagan took a job emceeing some shows in Las Vegas. It paid well and helped pay the bills but he hated the work, the environment. And Nancy too helped out by accepting a role in a movie.

In 1954 Reagan was hired to emcee G.E. Theater. It immediately became one of the most popular shows on television. As early as November it was topping "I Love Lucy" in the ratings.

As host Reagan traveled the country, making as many as fifteen speeches a day. "A typical day," he wrote, "would include a press conference at noon, a campus appearance at a high school, or college; six to fourteen meetings with industry employees and an evening banquet. I was on my feet in front of a microphone for 250,000 minutes."

But he learned something from these travels and it was in essence this: The workers were fed up with all the state regulations and they hated the high taxation. At first his speeches emphasized the company, and its pursuit of a

GOD and Ronald Reagan
God moves in the affairs of men

quality product and its concern for its employees, but, after spending hours talking to the average working stiff, he began to integrate the worker's concern and their wants.

And Reagan knew how to phrase their feelings in wonderful short and humorous sentences. On taxation: "If it moves tax it. If it keeps moving, regulate it. And if it stops moving, subsidize it."

Another one, which drew a rush of laughter, was in regard to the innate wisdom of the bureaucrats, with their sign on the colossal Hoover Dam. And the sign read: "GOVERNMENT PROPERTY. DO NOT REMOVE!"

In his view the most dangerous words in the English language were: "Hi, I'm from the government and I'm here to help!"

Reagan filled his speeches with humorous anecdotes of government waste and government miscues. He test marketed his speech as he traveled around the country. He captured the social and political philosophy of mid-America, the backbone of the country, and used it to promote his own philosophy.

* * * * * *

On July 25, 1962 his mother, Nelle died. She was seventy-nine. Reagan inherited her leather bound Bible. It was wonderfully old and wonderfully worn, literally embossed with his mother's fingerprints. There were notations in the margins, words underlined, phrases carefully marked.

For Reagan it was a treasure. It brought back distant memories; memories of his childhood; a childhood of happiness. They were poor, but "we never knew we were poor." Nelle created his world, a world of optimism, of faith, not only in God, but in the human spirit: That men of righteousness will prevail.

Harry von Bulow

"Never let life's problems destroy your ideals," she preached, and her voice echoed in his mind. The words were so familiar. And "Good will always triumph over evil."

And, of course, Reagan's own providential theology agreed with his mother's. "I always believed that we were, each of us, put here for a reason; that there is a place, a divine plan for all of us."

In 1964 Reagan's personal appearances were becoming more and more in demand. His pleasant mellifluous voice and memorable phrases captured the heart of millions of Americans.

At the time Goldwater's campaign funds were drying up. He needed money and needed it badly. He asked Reagan to appear on national television. The speech was designed to help finance Goldwater's bid for the presidency. Its reception was fabulous, producing over six million dollars in contributions to the Goldwater campaign fund.

This speech also changed Reagan's career. He visualized for himself a more challenging role; a more demanding goal. And a chance for him to initiate a new philosophy; a philosophy found only in the Scriptures; found only in his mother's Bible.

GOD and Ronald Reagan
God moves in the affairs of men

CHAPTER VIII

On January 4, 1966 Ronald Reagan announced his candidacy for the governorship of California.

Governor Brown was ecstatic. His opponent was a dunce, a nincompoop. "We'll have no trouble defeating this boob." And with wonderful and endearing confidence he roamed the State of California, tossing the California taxpayers' money here and there to ingratiate his staunch supporters. "This is going to be a runaway!" he chimed.

The political pundits and intellectuals agreed with Brown, calling Reagan a "Dummy, a faker, a kook and a dangerous man."

They didn't like his ideas, nor background. First, he was an actor; a Hollywood actor. "A plastic man with a cellophane brain," they said. And second, "He was a religious lunatic" (Christian).

"I not only have a strong faith in God," Reagan said, "but also faith in the common man."

Harry von Bulow

And that disturbed the intellectual and the cynical press.

And then he said, "I'm not sure I even believe in evolution."

This shocked the university community. They exploded, "He doesn't believe in evolution!"

One professor at Cal responded. "He must believe in Santa Claus."

"Or the Stork Theory!" exclaimed the Biology Prof at UCLA.

"How about the Easter Bunny!"

Reagan just smiled.

But Reagan had a star-studded campaign entourage. It included some of Hollywood's most glamorous stars, such as Frank Sinatra, Dean Martin, Bob Hope, John Wayne and Pat Boone. They toured the state. They sang, they danced, they endorsed Reagan in glowing terms. It was a Hollywood extravaganza. And everybody loved it, including some democrats and a load of independents sitting on the fence. In the meantime they made television commercials on his behalf.

While this was going on Deaver and Hannaford increased the radio coverage. Reagan was now heard on hundreds of radio stations in California, from tiny 100 Watters to 50,000 Watts. And the voters liked what they heard.

And Reagan won in a landslide!

* * * * * *

Ronald Wilson Reagan was inaugurated January 2, 1967 as Governor of California.

It was a gloomy day in Sacramento. It had rained the night before. The streets were wet and dirty. The cars were caked with mud and there was slush on the ground.

GOD and Ronald Reagan
God moves in the affairs of men

"It's a lousy day for an inauguration," commented Mike Deaver.

Sinatra agreed with him. "Why they put the capitol here, I'll never know." He paused and stared at the gray mist still in the air. "Malibu, or Santa Barbara would be a helluva lot better."

Then just as the new governor stepped to the podium, the black, ragged stratus clouds seem to part and a banner of sunlight beamed down on the podium, bathing the governor in a warm bit of golden light.

Nancy noticed it immediately. She had seen him in the limelight many times before; in Hollywood, at Los Vegas, but this seemed different. There were no stage lights, no one was working a spotlight. The light had just come through the clouds, as if a hand had swept away the dark, ragged clouds for a moment and let the warm sunlight englobe the new governor.

Sinatra pointed to the sky and smiled.

George Murphy welcomed the moment of warm sunlight. He nodded to Frank.

But after the governor's speech the sun faded behind the dark clouds, and once again the city was gray with rain and a cool wind shipped across the capitol grounds.

* * * * * *

There were a number of surprises that greeted the Reagan family when they came to Sacramento. First, they expected the governor's mansion to be livable. Apparently the former Governor and his family had lived there and survived, however, their survival may have been more for a political reason, than a poetical one.

The house was a three-story mansion, built in 1887. Except for some painting and a new roof now and then,

Harry von Bulow

little had been done inside to improve its livability. The house was a firetrap. None of the fireplaces worked and the Reagans were warned by the City Fire Chief not to use them for if they did, they may set the house on fire. And, of course, there were no fire escapes. They didn't use them in 1887, but they did have ropes in the upper rooms, so if there was a fire, you could open the window, toss out the rope and shinny down the side. This probably would have worked for Tom Mix, or Hoot Gibson, but it didn't seem too plausible for Nancy Reagan. And, at that time, they had two small children.

"And what should we do with them?" she asked the fire chief.

It was a good question and the fire chief didn't seem to have an answer.

The whole thing scared the hell out of her!

The house was made for Frankenstein: three stories filled with cold, drafty rooms; crammed with ancient voices; and windows covered by old, dark, velvet drapes ready to crumble into dust. To Nancy it had all the macabre of a funeral parlor. At any moment, she expected Boris Karloff to pop in.

For the children's safety and Nancy's mental health, they decided to move, but their political friends frowned on the idea.

"You'll destroy your career," they said.

"You can't leave the governor's mansion even though it might be a fire hazard."

"Might be!" said Reagan. "It is a fire hazard!"

"They'll think you're just another fancy dan from Hollywood. Too good to live in an old house in Sacramento."

Reagan shook his head and then said, "I can't jeopardize my family in a house that is a fire hazard, regardless of it being the governor's mansion or not." And

GOD and Ronald Reagan
God moves in the affairs of men

then as if putting a finale to the scene: "We're moving!" And they rented another house in Sacramento.

* * * * * *

About this time the "free speech" movement began in Berkeley and spread throughout the country. It was fueled by radical students in opposition to the Vietnam War. They ransacked the college campuses, damaged public buildings, urinated on government paintings, set fire to anything that would burn, and generally stopped the education of the student body.

It was still raging when Reagan became governor.

Clark Kerr, president of the University of California, symbolized the problem. He refused to discipline the student activists. Throughout this campus revolution he remained in his plush office and watched the festivities. He was either scared to death of them, or quietly endorsing their violent behavior.

Reagan was furious!

He announced his first target at a meeting at the Ambassador Hotel in Los Angeles. "In all the sound and fury at Berkeley, one voice is missing. And since it is the voice of those who built the university and pay the entire cost of the operation, I think it's time that voice was heard."

Governor Reagan was, of course, referring to the SDS (Students for a Democratic Society) strike against the U.S. Navy recruitment on the Berkeley Campus.

The Governor continued. "No one is compelled to attend the university. Those who do attend should accept and obey the prescribed rules, or pack up and get out!"

The next day he announced to his aides: "We're going to Berkeley."

Ed Meese advised against it.

Harry von Bulow

Mike Deaver was not enthused about the idea either. "It's too dangerous," he said.

But Reagan was not going to be intimidated by a bunch of rowdy, radical student protesters.

* * * * * *

As the governor's limousine rolled up to the Student's Union at Berkeley mobs of angry, swearing students crowded around it. They wiggled their fingers at the governor through the windows of the car; they spit on the car and booed the governor as he stepped out of the limousine. For a moment he stood and looked calmly at the jeering students. Some of them looked old enough to be his brother; some looked like girls, their hair hanging to their shoulders. And some wore beads and earrings like African natives and they screamed like Zulus on the warpath. This was higher education at Berkeley. He noticed the stuffed figure of himself burning near one of the buildings and then in the distance near the Bell Tower an American flag was set afire. It was quite a macabre scene, something that Joseph Conrad might write.

Then the State Patrolmen opened a wedge through the surging mob. It was not easy. The students pushed and shoved and swore and threw books and beer cans at them. But the patrolmen patiently persevered. Reagan was led into the Student's Union, where he stood on the podium and tried to make a speech, the raucous students making it virtually impossible for him to talk. They booed, yelled and jeered; their screaming voices shutting out his voice.

He ultimately stepped down from the podium, finally frustrated. "They're like mosquitoes and flies," he said. "They're part of the world, and you have to put up with them, I guess."

GOD and Ronald Reagan
God moves in the affairs of men

Meanwhile, President Kerr, relaxed in his office suite, studying the words of some esoteric cleric by the name of Ouusterbann. He seemed little concerned about the melee occurring outside. The sun cast a quiet beam of light into his study, lighting a new, leather-bound collection of Shakespeare's works.

* * * * * *

Watching the riots at Berkeley on television; hearing the screaming students, seeing the anger on their faces and feeling the violence in their hearts, Nancy became fearful of Ronnie's safety. She knew he had received numerous death threats and she became afraid that some crazy one might try to kill him. He was so vulnerable; so indifferent to danger!

Reagan called up the National Guard and they quickly quelled the riots. Peace finally reigned in Berkeley.

* * * * * *

Clark Kerr was dismissed as the President of the University of California on January 20, 1967.

Reagan, as governor, presided at the meeting. He said very little, sitting quietly, with pencil in hand doodling: his pencil moved slowly over the clean, white paper. Was he taking notes of the meeting, jotting down some profound remarks or comments? The pencil moved with artistic dexterity: first a long horse-like nose, then tall pointed ears, next a nice round rump. It was a jackass.

The regents of the University of California voted fourteen to eight in favor of Kerr's dismissal.

When the decision was announced and then flung out to the world by the New York Times, the Washington

Harry von Bulow

Post, the AP, the UP, the INS, the liberals screamed like wild banshees.

"He's killed our educational system!"

"The country's going to hell!"

"The greatest educational system in the whole world is being destroyed!"

"How could he do that to Kerri!"

And Reagan was the culprit. He was the demon who destroyed it. He was Mr. Beezlebub himself. The fourteen California Regents who voted for Kerr's dismissal were never mentioned.

"Reagan! The Hollywood nut was to blame!"

* * * * * *

There was another little surprise for Reagan when he reached Sacramento. Former Governor Brown had forgotten to mention that he had run the State of California into a six hundred million dollar deficit. This came to light one night as Reagan and his coterie studied the books.

This presented a new problem: Reagan did not want to tax the people of California more – they were taxed enough already, so he sent a clean, clear, white and black memo to the different departments in the state bureaucracy. It read: "Reduce operating expenses fifteen percent." This was met with the same bravado as the rioting students at Berkeley.

"Who in the hell does he think he is!" stormed the bureaucrats.

"We're down to bare bones already!"

"He's going to starve our families!"

Their anger shook the great stone buildings along the great white way in Sacramento.

But Reagan insisted.

GOD and Ronald Reagan
God moves in the affairs of men

Then came welfare. Reagan was in favor of helping only those in dire need. And he discussed his proposals with his cabinet.

"I want to know what each of you think of our chances of getting this thing through." It involved some seventy-seven proposals of welfare reform.

Their answer was almost unanimous: "None!" they said.

Another courageous fellow said, "We shouldn't even try."

Reagan looked around the room. Gloom had settled on the faces of this cabinet.

"Well, we're not going to get any reform unless we try."

Robert Carlson, his new Director of Welfare, ordered the production of an executive "blue book", which contained the proposals of the executive committee. And Bob Carlson had the honor of presenting this epistle to the democratic legislature. He first discussed it with James R. Mills, who was President Pro Tem of the Senate. Mr. Mills did not have time to read it. And when Bob Carlson asked the "very important" Mr. Mills if the governor could present it personally to the Senate. Mills said flatly: "Not on your life!"

Bob Carlson then went to the Speaker of the House, Mr. Morretti. He was greeted with the same sweet song: "Go to hell!"

Carlson immediately reported the response back to Governor Reagan. The governor smiled, but didn't seem concerned with their insolence. Instead he promptly made arrangements to go on state television. If Mills and Morretti wouldn't let him speak, he would talk directly to the millions of California voters, who would.

The speech began: "Here in California nearly a million children are growing up in the stultifying

Harry von Bulow

atmosphere of programs that reward people for not working, programs that separate families and doom these children to repeat the cycle in their own adulthood."

Then he gave examples of the rampant corruption in the system. One recipient drove her new Cadillac to the welfare office to pick up her check. I think she lived in Beverly Hills. Another family sent their son to Harvard on welfare payments; another did most of her shopping at Sak's Fifth Avenue.

He also called for the 230,000 absentee fathers to be pursued and persecuted and taught the responsibility of family life.

Soon Mr. Morretti began to feel the heat. And James Mills searched his wastebasket for the governor's seventy-seven welfare proposals. And Mr. Morretti with his head bowed and chomping a little crow, headed for the governor's office.

The two men produced one of the best and fairest welfare programs in the country, but it took a little time – a few months to pass. After all most legislators are lawyers.

In fact, over 87% of the California Legislators were attorneys. And, as you know attorneys love to talk and love to write and, to an attorney, nothing is simple. If the written law is not as thick as a Sears Catalog, something may be wrong; they may have missed something; forgot to dot an "i", cross a "t". Like the scribes of old they masticated, masturbated and massaged every word, every phrase of the welfare act. Like a cow chewing its cud they digested it and regurgitated it until they thought it was perfect. After weeks of cogitation they named it The California Welfare Reform Act.

It was finally approved by the California Legislature, all 807 pages of it, on August 13, 1971. It provided more money to those who really needed it and still saved the State over eight hundred million dollars.

GOD and Ronald Reagan
God moves in the affairs of men

Reagan's final comment: "Laws should be written by laymen, not lawyers. Things would be a lot simpler."

* * * * * *

And as governor Reagan simplified a lot of things, including his system of administration. He insisted that no issue was so complex that it couldn't be defined on one single page. He suggested four paragraphs: (1) State the problem. (2) Detail the facts. (3) List items to discuss. (4) Recommend a course of action.

He felt every government agency should follow the same procedure.

* * * * * *

To most everyone Reagan appeared as a friendly gentle man, like the fella' next door, the guy you sat next to at the local barbershop, or talked about the Ram-Green Bay game on Sunday. He just seemed to be some average guy. Nothing fancy. Nothing special.

In fact, one true story tells of a soldier fighting in Vietnam. He sent a money order to Governor Reagan. He wanted the governor to purchase some flowers for his wife on their anniversary.

Reagan showed the money order to Nancy.

"Thoughtful," said Nancy.

"And he sent me the money to buy them with," said Reagan. "What kind do you think she'd like?"

"Roses," said Nancy. "Red, red roses." Then he paused and added, "And nice card."

Governor Reagan not only went out and bought a dozen of red roses, but delivered them himself.

Harry von Bulow

When the young woman opened the door and sighted the governor, she was so stunned she could hardly speak.

And when he handed her the roses and card, she didn't know what to do.

But a smile and a soft word from the Governor relaxed her anxiety. "He must love you every much," said Reagan.

She nodded and accepted the flowers.

On another occasion an old man of about eighty years of age wrote the governor. "The wind is cold and I do not have a coat to wear."

That afternoon Nancy found him shuffling around in his closet.

"What are you doing?" Nancy seemed puzzled.

"I have a lot of extra stuff here," he said. "I thought I would get rid of it. I never wear it. I thought of giving some of it to the Salvation Army or to someone who needs it."

"If you'd wait, I could put some of my things in there, too."

"Good. Just put them on the pile."

"Need a bag?"

"That would help."

Nancy got a bag and started stuffing some of her things in. She was about to put an old overcoat into the bag, when Reagan stopped her.

"I'll take that," he said.

"You want to keep it?"

"No," he shook his head. "I know a fellow who needs one."

"Do we know him?"

"No, we don't know him."

"You got another letter?"

GOD and Ronald Reagan
God moves in the affairs of men

He handed her the letter. She read it slowly. "You going to deliver it personally?"

"Possibly."

She shook her head. "Have John take it." (He was the governor's chauffeur.) "The last time you made a personal delivery you almost scared the wits out of a mother."

Needless to say, John delivered the coat.[1]

Nelle, Reagan's mother, would have quoted Luke 3:10: "He that hath two coats, let him impart one to him that hath none."

Reagan knew the verse too, but he did not quote it aloud to Nancy.

The average guy, the dock worker, the carpenter, the cab driver, the housewife with a baby in her arms, the gas station attendant, the policeman on his beat, or the Army private all found a unique and strange affinity with this man. He was like someone they had known for a long time; a friend from the past they could trust and have faith in.

And multitudes followed Jesus. The rich man looked on from a distance, the intelligentsia made derogatory remarks, but the man in the street, the common man followed him along the hills of Judea and down to the Sea of Galilee.

Reagan may have appeared as a simple man, but beneath that visage was a revolutionary, who, like Christ, intended to change the existing order.

* * * * * *

---

[1] These were not publicity stuns pulled by a politician. Nancy and Ronnie never mentioned them to the press at the time. Only years later, when Nancy wrote her book "My Turn" did she write about these unusual happenings.

Harry von Bulow

The Vietnam war was slowly coming to an end. Governor Reagan held prayer breakfasts for the returning servicemen. One of those was a Navy pilot named John McCain. He had just been released as a prisoner of war and was on crutches.

Reagan had clearly expressed his anger with Kennedy and Johnson for waging a war they had never planned to win. Impossible restrictions were put on our troops: The Air Force couldn't fly beyond a certain parallel and the infantry were limited to a certain number of bullets they could fire. This was a war run by politicians in Washington, D.C. and Reagan hated the war, the people running it and the politicians promoting it.

A military couple wrote the governor: "You have our two votes for any office in the land."

After the Vietnam debacle there came the Watergate Scandal. The break-in occurred on June 17, 1972, but hung on like a vulture until August 9, 1974 when Nixon finally resigned.

On January 3, 1975 Reagan ended his eight years as Governor of California and returned to his home in Pacific Palisades. In the meantime, he had purchased a ranch north of Santa Barbara.

GOD and Ronald Reagan
God moves in the affairs of men

CHAPTER IX

Michael Deaver and Pete Hannaford opened a public relations firm in Los Angeles. Ronald Reagan was their sole client, however, they did not mention it to Reagan. They went ahead and sold his services as writer, speaker, and broadcaster. They lined up over one hundred radio stations and almost as many newspapers to carry the former governor's current affairs commentary.

Finally Deaver telephoned Reagan at the ranch and informed him what they had done.

Reagan was not pleased. He was happy on his beautiful ranch north of Santa Barbara. He had named it "Rancho del Cielo", a ranch in the clouds. It had seven hundred acres of rolling hills and rugged terrain. And an old adobe house, which resembled more of a shack than a home. But he and Nancy loved it. They would fix up the house, add a few rooms, a nice barn for their horses, enlarge the fireplace. And he could ride the range, gulp in clean, fresh air and sharpen his ax and cut some trees and timber to warm their hearth. And get in shape. He hated the

73

Harry von Bulow

sedentary life. He loved the out-of-doors. He felt free and closer to God and nature.

Deaver was concerned. "You can't quit now," he said.

"You should see this place," said Reagan. "It's like living on a cloud."

"We have over a hundred radio stations ready to take your show."

Reagan ignored him, but continued his description of the ranch. "It's like looking down on the world. You've never seen anything like it."

"And a hundred conservative newspapers," added Hannaford.

"I can ride for miles around this place," continued Reagan, "in any direction."

There was a long pause, and Deaver said, "Remember that dream, Ron?"

Reagan did not reply.

"The one where you're living in a white house with tall columns?"

Reagan thought a long time, as if recalling the dream. Then he said and this quite firmly, "I don't care if I ever see another executive desk."

That seemed to be the finale. Deaver said goodbye and hung up, then turned to Hannaford.

"Pete, I don't think he's interested."

"What are we going to do with those one hundred stations and newspapers?"

"Tell them we're still in the planning stage." And then Deaver scratched his head, loosened his tie, and shrugged his shoulders. "Tell them anything you can think of."

* * * * * *

GOD and Ronald Reagan
God moves in the affairs of men

A few months later, when he and Mike Deaver were flying from San Francisco to Los Angeles, a little, old lady recognized Reagan.

"Governor Reagan?" And she had to bend her head back to talk to him. She must not have been over five feet tall.

He bent down and smiled. "Yes," he said.

"I'm so happy to meet you," and her tiny, but strong, little hand grasped his hand firmly. "You're my favorite!"

Reagan smiled.

But the little woman (she must have been at least eighty) was not through, and she continued to hold his hand and then she finally said, "You gotta run for President!"

She tapped his hand affectionately. "God bless you." And then she smiled and walked back to her seat in the plane.

Reagan rejoined Deaver and for a while just stared out the window of the plane. It seemed like such a pleasant ride down the California coast: The beautiful beaches, the dark, rugged mountains in the distance and the white cumulus clouds casting a moving shadow on the beaches below.

Finally Reagan turned to Deaver.

"Mike," he began, "I guess I really do have to run."

Deaver smiled and then exclaimed, "It's time for me to get into the game!"

And when the plane landed in Los Angeles, Deaver raced for the first phone booth he saw and called his partner, Hannaford.

"Pete," he said, almost shouting into the phone. "He's going to run!"

Hannaford could hardly believe what he had heard.

"Get the ball rollin'!" exploded Deaver.

Harry von Bulow

* * * * * *

And the "ball started rollin'". Some 350 radio stations were signed up, reaching an audience of ten to fifteen million people every time he spoke.

President Ford was becoming concerned. He tried to distract Reagan with appointments. "Would you serve on the Rockefeller Commission, or would you rather become a member of the cabinet. Maybe Secretary of Commerce."

Reagan refused them all, except the Rockefeller Commission. He did accept that one, but he didn't want to become a part of Ford's cabinet. Their philosophy he knew clashed with his. He wanted no part of the Ford Cabinet.

Reagan thought he had a good chance of winning the Republican nomination for the presidency in 1976.

By the middle of 1970, following the Vietnam War, the Democrats had become a party of disarmament. They believed that a détente with the Reds was the only way to go. Regardless of whether the Russians ever obeyed the treaties seemed insignificant to them. But, they said, at least it kept some sort of peace. And the Republicans couldn't think of any other way to go, so they went along with the Democrats.

So, when Reagan attacked détente as futile, the liberal press began its war with Reagan: He was a warmonger, a dangerous man, a wildman from the west that could not be trusted to keep the peace, a fragile peace that was setting on a time bomb. In the meantime, Russia was expanding its arsenal of nuclear weapons.

Reagan announced his intentions of running for the presidency at the National Press Club in Washington, D.C. James Reston of the New York Times reflected the general feeling of the press, when he wrote: "...amusing, but frivolous. A Reagan fantasy."

GOD and Ronald Reagan
God moves in the affairs of men

Later that day Reagan flew to Miami. First stop, an airport rally. As Reagan was speaking a voice in the crowd called out "Hey Dutch!" He knew it was somebody from Iowa, where Reagan had been a sports announcer at WHO.

"Hi there!" Reagan called back. "I'll come to see you when I'm done."

When Reagan finished speaking, one of the secret service agents said, "When you leave the platform, turn to your left."

Instead Reagan turned to his right to look for his friend. But a moment later, Tommy Thomas, Reagan's chairman in Florida, yelled, "What the hell do you think you're doing!" Tommy plunged into the crowd and a moment later, he and two other men were wrestling a dark haired young man to the ground. The man was holding a gun and it took three of them to get him down. As it turned out, the gun was a toy, but looked exactly like a forty-five revolver.

Later, Nancy told Ronny and with firmness in her voice. "From now on if the Secret Service men say turn left, you turn left! Do what they tell you to do."

Nancy was shaking and Ronnie put his arm around her and calmed her down.

The first primary was held in New Hampshire and Ford won by 1,317 votes. With momentum in his favor he won in Florida, Massachusetts, Vermont and Illinois.

For a moment it looked like a runaway for Ford. The Post asked, "When are you going to get our of the race?"

But then Reagan won in North Carolina, Texas, Georgia, Alabama and Indiana.

The former chairman of the Republican National Committee endorsed Ford.

On March 17th the National Republican Conference of Mayors asked Reagan to withdraw.

Harry von Bulow

The L.A. Times wrote: "Time to bow out, Reagan."

On the 20th the Republican Governors issued a statement calling for Reagan to quit.

The Ford machine was beginning to show its power, carefully orchestrating these demands.

Reagan ignored them and kept plowing along. The only support he had from the Republican Party was Paul Laxalt of Nevada.

Then his "Friend" Barry Goldwater, the man he had vigorously supported in '72 and raised over six million dollars for in campaign funds, announced his support for Gerald Ford. This was a heart-felt blow to Reagan. He had thought Goldwater was his friend. He didn't expect him to endorse his opponent. But Reagan accepted it without a derisive word and quietly headed for the convention. Regardless of the news media and the power of the president, Reagan still was almost even in votes as the convention began.

But sometimes strange things happen in dark corners and smoky rooms and Washington latrines. All at once, quite mysteriously in fact, some of Reagan's supporters started feeling certain political pressures. Al Capone would have called it blackmail. Ma Reagan would have called it an abomination.

But it worked. Legal, or illegal Ford won the nomination.

* * * * * *

In a cold, bleak ballroom Thursday morning, Reagan delivered his valedictory to his anguished staffers. Some of them were in tears; all were completely exhausted, but it was obvious they all loved him and would have battled up San Juan Hill, or any other hill if he had asked them.

GOD and Ronald Reagan
God moves in the affairs of men

He began: "The individuals on this stage may change, but the cause is there and the cause will prevail because it is right." He paused, studied the faces of his supporters. "Don't get cynical," he said, although everyone in the room knew that the nomination had been stolen from him by a naked, last minute exercise of White House power.

But Reagan tried to lighten up the dreary occasion with a bit of humor: "Someone once described backstage politics as a little bit like looking at civilization with its pants down." But he was having trouble trying to control his own emotions. The final words were almost tear-stained. "Don't give up your ideals. Recognize that there are millions and millions of Americans out there who want what you want...a shining city on a hill." And he waved and they cheered and he left the stage.

The phrase hung in his mind like a shadow from the past. He could hear his mother Nelle repeating it, only it was slightly different. It was "a city set on a hill cannot be hid," or was it "Ye are the light of the world." Both from Matthew 5. It was strange how his mother had become so much a part of his life, his actions; even his writing and speaking.

He turned to Nancy.

"Let's get out of here," she said. "It's depressive." And she grabbed his hand and they left.

* * * * * *

That evening Nancy and he sat in his high, glassed-in box overlooking the convention. It was an acceptable location but a long way from the podium. They sat quietly watching Ford make his acceptance speech.

Tom Brokaw, an NBC reporter, stuck his nose into the Reagan box. "Will you go down on the platform with President Ford?"

Harry von Bulow

Reagan shook his head, no. "I have no desire to go down there."

Ford droned on, his dreary technique had all the drama of a toadstool. With sweat pouring off his brow, he ended his speech as the hall applauded him. Then he began waving wildly at the distant glass box in an attempt to get Reagan's attention, but Reagan only smiled and then looking at Nancy he said, "It's his night. I'm not going down there."

The band started to play, but Ford shouted above it, "Ron, will you come down and bring Nancy?"

All eyes in the hall were focused on the glass box where Reagan sat and a steady chant began to reverberate throughout the great hall, "We want Ron! We want Ron!" And the band caught the tempo and soon the place was shaking with "We want Ron! We want Ron!" and all put to music.

John Chancellor, peering through high-powered field glasses spotted the Reagans. "They're beginning to move," he said and then, "They may be going down the hallway."

On stage President Ford and his running mate, Dole waited. They waited. And waited. And Ford sweating profusely grabbed Dole's hand and began waving it in the air. Betty Ford and her three children, Elizabeth Dole and Nelson Rockefeller all were smiling. Smiling. Waiting. Smiling. They wondered if the Reagans had gotten lost in the bowels of the building. It seemed forever before they arrived on stage.

Reagan finally appeared, his tall, relaxed, handsome figure moving gracefully across the stage, as the crowd applauded and shouted, "We want Ron. We want Ron!" Ford was still sweating profusely. At that moment, he wondered why he was there, instead of Reagan. The band swung into "California Here I Come" and Reagan broke

GOD and Ronald Reagan
God moves in the affairs of men

into a broad smile, while Ford stood stricken and stone-faced. Was this his convention or Reagan's? Now he was not sure.

As the music "California Here I Come" came to a close, Ford stepped to the podium and invited Governor Reagan to say a few words.

"Thank you Mr. President, Mrs. Ford, Mr. Vice President and Mr. Vice President to be...those of you watching from a distance, all of those millions of Democrats and independents, who I know are looking for a cause around which to rally and which I believe we can give them."

Ford moved towards the podium. He thought Reagan was about through.

But Reagan had just begun. "I believe the Republican Party has a platform that is a banner of bold, unmistakable colors with no pale pastel shades." And then he began to tell a story: "Someone asked me to write a letter for a time capsule that is going to be opened in Los Angeles a hundred years from now, on our Tricentennial. It sounded like an easy assignment. They suggested I write something about the problems and issues of the day. I set out to do so, riding down the Coast in an automobile, looking at the blue Pacific out on one side and the Santa Ynez Mountains on the other, and I couldn't help but wonder if it was going to be that beautiful a hundred years from now.

"And suddenly I thought to myself, if I write of the problems, they will be the domestic problems of which the President spoke here tonight, the challenges confronting us, the erosion of freedom, that has taken place under Democratic rule in this country, the invasion of private rights, the controls and restrictions on the vitality of the great, free economy that we enjoy. These are the challenges that we must meet."

Harry von Bulow

Ford stood silently behind the podium, his face drawn and gloomy, realizing that his own speech had been merely a warm-up for this one.

"And then again there is the challenge of which he spoke, that we live in a world in which the great powers aimed at each other horrible missiles of destruction, nuclear weapons that can in a matter of minutes arrive at each other's country and destroy virtually the civilized world we live in.

"And suddenly, it dawned on me, those who read this letter a hundred years from now will know whether those missiles were fired. They will know whether we met our challenge. Whether they can have the freedom that we have known up until now will depend on what we do here.

"Will they look back with appreciation and say, "Thank God for those people in 1976 who headed off that loss of freedom, who kept us now a hundred years later free, who kept our world from nuclear destruction."

By now, hundreds of faces in the audience were wet with tears. And then in finale: "This is our challenge; and this is why...we must go forth from here united, determined that what a great general said a few years ago is true: there is no substitute for victory, Mr. President."

The roar that followed this stirring speech dwarfed any heard before.

"Beautiful...just beautiful!" Rockefeller seized Reagan's hand in congratulations.

Then Reagan and his lovely Nancy, beautifully dressed in a cool white evening gown, glided off the stage, leaving an awkward, silent cavity. Ford and Dole tried to fill it with smiles and waving of arms, but the convention was over. And their hero had gone. Santa Claus had left; the Easter Bunny had gone; the parade was over. And the convention had picked the wrong man.

GOD and Ronald Reagan
God moves in the affairs of men

CHAPTER X

James Earl Carter, known to his friends as Jimmy, was the personification of youth and health compared to his opponent Gerald Ford. Carter was supposed to be smarter, too; graduating in the upper third of his class at the Naval Academy. His countenance was pope-like and ingratiating, except when he smiled, then he showed a row of dull, buck teeth. Although he spoke slowly, with sort of a lazy southern accent, he was a tough, persistent campaigner. His Navy background created an aura of leadership and courage. With memories of America's most gallant naval heroes...Perry, Halsey and Nimitz, the voters hoped and prayed Carter would follow in their footsteps.

Gerald Ford, on the other hand, had inherited his power when Nixon resigned. The Watergate Scandal still permeated Washington and some of its odor still clouded the Ford campaign. Ford was a great football player at Michigan, but his leather helmet probably caused early balding and a more aged appearance; nor was he the most charismatic person on the planet. In fact, he had a rather

Harry von Bulow

dull, monotonous speaking voice and the countenance of an Egyptian mummy.

Carter won the election and Gerald Ford headed for Palm Springs and his wife to a sanitarium for a drinking problem.

* * * * * *

Carter arrived at the White House on a high note, when he stepped out of his limousine and walked down Pennsylvania Avenue with his pretty wife by his side. The crowd loved it. They laughed and cheered as he passed them by. It was an inspiring moment. He seemed to be joining, allying himself with the common folk, who lined the avenue.

And he did prove to be very much like them. For Carter's outlook for America was very much like the grocery clerk's. His vision for the country was limited, finite. He felt America had reached its peak; that now we must save, conserve our resources, "Batten-down-the-hatch" as an old Navy man might have put it. According to the new president the U.S. had seen its best days. He cancelled the building of supersonic transports, issued bills for White House hospitality, public lights were dimmed, and the heat was turned off in the White House. He put on long underwear during the winter months, and gave away the Panama Canal. In the meantime fifty-two American hostages were taken prisoner in Iran.

Carter was trying to run the federal government like he ran his peanut farm. And it didn't work. In fact, his leadership was leading the country into a quagmire, a dead end. Even the military was inept. The economy was swirling down the drain. Interest rates were soaring to eighteen and twenty percent. Nobody could afford a house. Food prices had doubled. Unemployment hovered around

GOD and Ronald Reagan
God moves in the affairs of men

ten percent. Economically the country was constipated. Nothing moved. It was lethargic.

And then Iran kidnapped fifty-two Americans and held them hostage for 440 days. This was the final straw. As a last resort he sent in a military mission, but even that was done inexpertly. It landed in a sand pile outside of Iran and the plane's motors were fouled up by blowing sand. The mission had to be scrubbed and eight men lost their lives.

It was obvious that the country, under Jimmy Carter had lost its way. Jimmy should have stayed home on the farm. He was great in overalls, or leading a donkey, but he was not a leader of men.

The country began looking for a leader, praying for a leader!

Then Reagan came on the scene.

Harry von Bulow

CHAPTER XI

As was expected Reagan was nominated at the Republican Convention of 1980. For his running mate he preferred his personal friend Paul Laxalt, but he was from a small state, with few electoral votes, or national power. Texas had all the assets.

Reagan turned to his friend, "Why in the hell did you have to live in Nevada?"

Lexalt smiled, "Good luck," he said.

The next night Reagan made his acceptance speech, making reference to the Carter years: "Can anyone compare the state of our economy and say 'Well done.' Can anyone look at our reduced standing in the world today, and say, 'Let's have four more years of this?' Can anyone look at the record of this administration and say, 'Well done?'"

And then he ended his speech on a note of inspiration, and when he was finished the crowd was completely still. Then he looked out on the convention floor and surprised everyone by saying, "I'll confess I've

GOD and Ronald Reagan
God moves in the affairs of men

been a little afraid to suggest what I am going to suggest, what I'm going to say. I'm more afraid not to. Can we begin our crusade joined together in a moment of silent prayer?"

The entire convention rose up and bowed their heads. After a few seconds, Reagan looked out on that great hall and said, "God bless America."

The next day the battle for the presidency began.

* * * * * *

The campaign's modus operandi was quite simple: Both Nancy and he would fly out on their plane named "Leadership 80". Once they reached their destination, we'll say Chicago Illinois for an example, Ronnie would campaign in the city of Chicago, while Nancy would go to the smaller markets around the state, like Sterling, or Dixon, or Fulton.

The plane, "Leadership '80", became not only a working office, but also a part of their entertainment. This sort of gave them a moment of relaxation from the tensions of campaigning, a rigorous and most demanding part of their lives. While in flight Nancy would pass out chocolates. Another game included Nancy rolling an orange down the center aisle of the plane. And, if the orange reached the end of the aisle without going under the seats, she could declare a victory. It was a crazy game, meaningless really, but it relieved the tenseness of their life. And the reporters kidded her and egged her on.

The pilot also kept a rubber chicken in the cockpit and, as they landed, he would stick it on the windshield of the plane and then he would radio the tower that they had evidently hit something on the way down. And, as the plane taxied to the runway, the man on the runway would be

Harry von Bulow

moving his arms slower and slower as he stared at the unidentified object on the plane's windshield.

Of course on these flights Reagan and his staff spent most of their time discussing strategy, working on speeches, doing interviews with the press and making plans for the next stop.

At first, there was some confusion; responsibilities had to be assigned, etc. Things started to smooth out when Stu Spencer arrived. He was an old friend of the Reagans and had been with them on the California campaigns.

In the early part of the campaign Reagan charged Carter with leading the country into a "depression".

Carter picked up the word "Depression" and retorted, "That shows how little he knows." And then he continued, "This is not a depression, but a recession."[1]

Reagan came back. "They say I can't use the word depression. Well, if the president wants a definition, I'll give him one. A recession is when your neighbor loses his job. A depression is when you lose your job. And recovery will be when Carter loses his."

On October 28 there was the Carter-Reagan Debate. This was just a few days before the election. In this debate Reagan turned to the audience and asked them a number of questions. "Are you better off than you were four years ago? Is it easier for you to go and buy things in the store than it was four years ago? Is there more or less employment? Is America as respected throughout the world as it was? Do you feel that our security is safe, that we're as strong as we were four years ago? If your answer to all these questions is yes, why I think your choice is obvious. If you don't agree, if you don't think that this course that we've been following for the past four years, then I would suggest another choice that you have."

---

[1] Campaign 1980

GOD and Ronald Reagan
God moves in the affairs of men

Intermittently there were hecklers and once in Brooklyn (probably an old Dodger fan) started yelling at him that he was a warmonger, that he wanted to start a war, but Reagan called back, "No, I don't want to do that. But if I did, I'd start right here with you guys!"

On the day of the election, now back home in California and going to a polling place that they had gone to for many years, the women put out jars of jelly beans for him.

And as they left, one reporter called out. "And what about your wife. Who did she vote for?"

Reagan smiled and then replied, "Oh, Nancy voted for some has-been actor."

On November 3, 1980, on the eve of the election, a rare and unique phenomenon occurred in the sky over Tampico, Illinois: A double rainbow appeared over his birthplace. No one in Tampico had seen anything like it before.

"It must be some kind of omen," said the mayor.

The Episcopal Vicar nodded, and said, "It is a good sign." And he quoted Genesis Chapter 9: 8-16, when the Great Genesis flood ended and God painted a beautiful rainbow in the sky. "It is a good sign," he repeated.

The longest day in the world is election day. Yet, that day, that year, was most unusual for Reagan was announced the winner as early as five o'clock in the afternoon in California. John Chancellor made the announcement: Reagan had won by a landslide!

In Dixon, Illinois a newsman at the little 250-Watt Radio Station WIXN announced in a pleasant, baritone voice. "The Rock River flows for you tonight, Mr. Ronald Reagan." He hesitated a moment, then rephrased it: "Mr. President."

Harry von Bulow

The telephone started ringing. It was former President Jimmy Carter calling to concede and to congratulate Ronald Reagan for his victory.

GOD and Ronald Reagan
God moves in the affairs of men

CHAPTER XII

"And he said, Verily I say unto you no
Prophet is accepted in his own country."

Luke 4: 23-27.

When Reagan arrived at the White House, it was like entering a battlefield. The only friends he had were Nancy, his wife, and about forty-four million voters. But in Washington that doesn't mean anything.

What is important is the news media, and the intellectual elite, who rule Washington.

To Hell with the voters!

Reagan was also the oldest man in U.S. history to gain the presidency. He was sixty-nine, but looked like forty-five.

Inauguration day was dark and dreary with stratus clouds hanging low over the capitol. There was dampness in the air, a feeling of rain or snow, although the temperature was in the low fifties.

Harry von Bulow

I think Nancy Reagan tells the story of the inauguration better than anyone else. The following is quoted from her book "My Turn."

"At 11:39 a.m., while the trumpets played 'Jubilant', Ronnie arrived on the podium. George Bush was sworn in first. Barbara held a Bible that had been given to them by Billy Graham, as Justice Porter Stewart administered the oath.

"Then it was Ronnie's turn. I stood beside him, holding the Reagan family Bible. It had belonged to Ronnie's mother, and inside she had listed the births and deaths in her family, the Wilson's. It was old and crumbling and taped together, and it seemed just right for the occasion.

"On the inside of the front cover, Nelle had written these words: 'A thought for today: You can be too big for God to use, but you cannot be too small'."

"Just before noon Chief Justice Warren Burger administered the oath and Ronnie repeated the words after him."

Then suddenly it was over. The president kissed his wife and a booming, thundering twenty-one-gun salute rang out in honor of the new president. Reagan shook the hand of former President Carter and then stepped to the podium to begin his inaugural address.

AT THIS MOMENT EVERYTHING CHANGED!

A writer from Time Magazine wrote: "As he (Reagan) raised his head to look out at the crowd, a strange and wonderful thing happened. The dark, cloudy sky over his head began to part slightly, within seconds there was a gaping hole in the gray overcast, and a brilliant, golden shaft of wintry sun burst through the clouds and bathed the inaugural stand and the watching crowd. As Reagan spoke a slight breeze ruffled his hair and the warm, golden light beamed down on him.

GOD and Ronald Reagan
God moves in the affairs of men

"Later, a few minutes after he finished speaking as if on cue from some master lighter backstage, the hole in the clouds shrank, the sky darkened and Washington grew gray and cold once again" (Time Magazine, January 1980).

Remember two thousand years ago. "And it came to pass in those days, that Jesus came from Nazareth and was baptized of John in the Jordan."
"And straightaway coming up out of the water, he saw the heavens opened and the Spirit like a dove descending upon him." (Mark 1:9-10)

Certainly Reagan was no Messiah, but he was, I believe, embraced by the Holy Spirit. Nelle, his mother, had instilled in him the teachings of Christ. And he believed implicitly in the Lord.

Nancy recalled the day in Sacramento long ago, when he was inaugurated Governor of California. It had been the same kind of day: cold, dreary, an icy drizzle fell on the city, but when Reagan got up to speak, the dark clouds parted and a banner of sunlight bathed the podium where the Governor was about to speak.

She wondered if this was an omen, a harbinger of good things to come.

* * * * * *

They moved inside of the Capitol for lunch. The children told Ronnie how proud they were and an enormous crush of well wishers tried to shake his hand and offer their congratulations.

Luncheon was with the Congressional leaders in the beautiful Statutory Hall. There were California roses on each table and all the ladies received a souvenir – a small silver-plated box filled with jellybeans.

93

Harry von Bulow

Toward the end of the lunch Reagan made the announcement everyone was waiting for: "With thanks to the Almighty God, I have been given a tag line, the get-off line everyone wants at the end of a toast, or speech: Some thirty minutes ago, the planes bearing our prisoners left Iranian air space and are free of Iran."

The guests immediately stood up, applauded and cheered.

"Thank God!" one shouted.

"Great!" shouted another.

It was, to say the least, a wonderful an happy occasion.

* * * * * *

It wasn't surprising for the eastern elite, or the intellectuals to hate Reagan. He was an "outsider". He wasn't a part of their "enlightened" group. He was the cactus in the rose garden. The dog pee on the new rug. And they hated him.

All at once the new president was a challenge to their entire world view. For it was this elite brain trust which had concocted the brilliant "containment" policy which balanced the power between the two most powerful nations in the world – Russia and the United States. It was this sensitive balance which, according to them, assured the world of peace in our time.

But, all at once, along comes this cornball from the Midwest named Reagan. And he is not only from a tiny town in Illinois, but he graduated from a college they had never heard of before: named Eureka College.

"Eureka!" exclaimed a professor from Princeton.

"Is it in Athens?" laughed another.

"In Dixon."

"Dixon?"

GOD and Ronald Reagan
God moves in the affairs of men

"It's in the Midwest. Illinois, or Iowa, or Indiana." The geography professor from Yale paused, then continued. "Some place among the rows of corn and barley."

"Dixon," said the professor from Harvard. "It rhymes with Nixon."

"Another calamity."

"Who's going to write his scripts in Washington?"

The professor shook his tousled head.

"He sure can read those cue cards good," laughed the woman from Time.

"Has a nice voice."

Pause.

"Eureka College," hummed the Yale professor. "I don't think that's in Dixon. I believe it is in DeKalb, Illinois."

"DeKalb?" The Harvard man was puzzled. "Is that an Indian tribe?"

"Sounds Indian."

"Did he major in basket weaving?"

"Or maybe tent making."

They were really enjoying themselves.

But there was another bomb waiting for these "intellectual giants." It would explode in the next few days and implode every tiny intellectual brain cell in Washington. It was a sort of Reagan Manifesto. It was this: Reagan was NOT going to pursue the policy of "containment" for Russia. Instead he was going to bring freedom, democracy and capitalism to the Soviet Union.

This was the final blow! For years these elite gentleman had ruled the world. They had advised Nixon, Carter, Eisenhower and Kennedy. They were the architects of U.S. foreign policy. Most of them considered themselves the brains behind the throne; the throne being the Oval Office. Now their power was being challenged.

95

Harry von Bulow

During most of Reagan's political life he had fought communism. At SAG, as president of the Screen Actor's Guild, he played a key role in blocking a communist takeover of the movie industry. As Governor of California he had battled the communists, who had infiltrated the California University System. Reagan was intimately acquainted with their modus operandi: He knew how they operated and how ruthless they could be. But he had defeated them on both occasions.

In essence, he was telling these gentlemen that they had lost faith in their country and mankind. Reagan knew that free men could out-produce slave labor: that men of faith could change Russia, defeat communism, collapse its economic system.

The Washington elite were stunned. They thought he was gullible and stupid. According to their wisdom nobody was going to change Russia. Only a fool would think so.

Arthur Schlesinger, Jr., (a close friend of the Kennedys) said, "Those who think the USSR will collapse are kidding themselves."

John Kenneth Galbraith (Certainly you've heard of him) said, "Russia is in better shape than the U.S."

Paul Samuelson (Who could be more brilliant!) of MIT commented, "The Soviet System is more efficient than the U.S."

And James Reston (A profound writer) of the New York Times: "The Soviet collapse is impossible!"

Lester Thurow (Certainly a wise man), famous economist wrote: "Its economic achievements rival those of the U.S."

And finally the brilliant Steven Cohn from Princeton popped in this little dandy: "Reagan is suffering from Sovieticus." Whatever that means.

GOD and Ronald Reagan
God moves in the affairs of men

* * * * * *

This Washington elite were like the rich and powerful Sadducees and Pharisees of Jesus time, who hated this man from Nazareth, for He could perform miracles, while they could not. And the common people in Judea followed Him and worshipped Him. And the high and mighty Sadducees and Pharisees saw their influence, their power over the people, declining. And they became angry and vindictive: "Has anything good ever come out of Nazareth?" they asked. And, "Is not this the carpenter's son?" Certainly they, the intellectuals and wise men of their world, were not going to let a carpenter's son usurp their power. And so they told the people: It is the work of Beezlebub, the devil.

And, when Reagan was elected president, the liberal snobs crowed loud and long. They wanted nothing to do with him. They hated him. He was Beezlebub, the devil to them.

Clark Clifford, a political potentate, roared, "He's an amiable dunce."

Michael Kinsley, a Karmelcorn columnist, wrote "Not terribly bright."

Robert Wright of the liberal, almost pink, Republic scribbled, "...virtually brain dead."

The storm trooper Nichola von Hoffman described him as "...a self assured bumpkin."

The Washington elite did not hang him on a tree, but they tried to crucify him with their angry, insulting invectives.

Harry von Bulow

Reagan only smiled, their so-called "wisdom" was only foolishness to him.[1]

* * * * * *

The Washington Post began the war with their Pulitzer Prize winning cartoonist, Herb Bloch. Bloch, with brilliant strokes of his brush, portrayed Reagan as a dunce, the pointed cap resting at an angle on the president's head. Other cartoons showed him snoozing in the oval office.

And the Times sent spies out to pick up strange idiosyncrasies the president may have had; any kind of tiny, or minute thing that made him look like a fool.

"This guy's from fairyland," said the Editor of the Time. Hollywood was frequently referred to as Fairyland. "I want you to follow this guy, wherever he goes and check everything he says."

"Like Dick Tracy."

"Like Dick Tracy," continued the editor. "If he makes mistakes; if he uses a double negative, or forgets a name, or a department, or farts in the White House I want to know about it.

"I take it you don't like him," said the reporter.

"Put it this way. I don't like Hollywood. I don't like their pretty looks, their soft voices, and above all, I don't like their bullshit." He paused and stared angrily at the reporter. "Got it!"

"Got it."

* * * * * *

And then there was the thing about his hair.

---

[1] I Corinthians, Chapter 2:14. "But the natural man receiveth not the things of the Spirit of God for they are foolishness unto him."

GOD and Ronald Reagan
God moves in the affairs of men

"What kind of hair coloring does he use?"

"He claims it's his natural hair."

"He's seventy-one, isn't he?"

"Something like that."

"Maybe he takes a pill."

"I don't know."

"Maybe it's one of those Reagan miracles!" And he laughed.

* * * * * *

He was the reigning monarch of the House. He was a round, fat man, about the size of a Japanese Summo wrestler. His name was "Tip" O'Neil. He had been around so long in the Washington world that he thought he owned the place.

He was not impressed by Reagan.

When President Reagan first met him, O'Neil addressed him as "Mr. President", but there was a noticeable slur in his voice.

Reagan ignored the insult.

"I've heard a great deal about you," said Reagan, being friendly and smiling.

O'Neil grunted.

Reagan continued. "I got along well with the Democratic Senate in California."

"This is Washington," said O'Neil.

Reagan smiled.

"You were in the minor leagues then," he continued, "You're in the majors now."

Reagan ignored O'Neil's surliness. "I think we should have lunch sometime soon."

O'Neil grunted again.

Still smiling Reagan said, "Thank you for your time, Mr. Speaker."

Harry von Bulow

* * * * * *

At times Reagan seemed invulnerable to criticism; like he was wearing armor, or there was some invisible shield protecting him. It was a time when his friends, or enemies wanted him to compromise his beliefs, or his ethics for some political gain, or worldly approbation. At that time, the shield went up. Reagan, like Lincoln, like Cromwell, like Washington, like every great leader, never compromised his ethics, nor beliefs for political gain.

Two thousand years ago the Apostle Matthew wrote: "With God all things are possible". Matthew 19:26.

Oliver Cromwell, one of the most courageous warriors of his time, felt the same way only he phrased it differently: "I fear no man. I fear only God."

And Abraham Lincoln: "Without assistance of that Divine Being, I cannot succeed. With his assistance I cannot fail."

And George Washington at Valley Forge: "We pray for food, warm clothing and victory. May the Lord grant them."

And Ronald Reagan: "I always believed that we were, each of us, put here for a reason; that there is a place, a divine plan for all of us."

All great leaders during the time of war or peace place their faith in the Almighty. Reagan always felt the Lord's presence and believed implicitly in the power of the Holy Spirit; that God would lead him through the wilderness in Washington, D.C. as well as throughout the world.

This faith had been instilled in him from the time he was a child. Nelle had read the Bible to him night after night and the wonderful Bible stories became his intimate companions. And as he grew up Christ became more and

GOD and Ronald Reagan
God moves in the affairs of men

more an integral part of his life. Its Christian ethnics and morals became the cornerstone and foundation of his character.

Harry von Bulow

CHAPTER XIII

Reagan spoke at the Washington Hilton and then left the hotel at 2:25 p.m., stepping through the side door. Accompanying him was his doctor, Michael Deaver, three Secret Service Agents and James Brady, Press Secretary to the President. The motorcade waited just about thirteen feet ahead, the motors humming; a knot of television and press reporters stood to his left as he headed for his limousine.

Then, as the president raised his arm to wave to the onlookers, a sharp, cracking sound penetrated the air. Suddenly everyone around him was moving, running, falling, Reagan was shoved into the limo, his head bumping the window frame, the Secret Service man was on top of him, protecting him. And as he glanced out the window he saw a blond bystander crouched and spraying bullets around.

"Haul ass!" a voice shouted. "Let's get out of here!!"

GOD and Ronald Reagan
God moves in the affairs of men

Now the limousine was speeding down Connecticut Avenue, then directed to George Washington University Hospital. Miraculously it reached the clinic in three and a half minutes.

He was placed on a gurney. Rushed to the Operating Room. His lungs started to congest with blood, he was beginning to suffocate.

"Get some oxygen into him!"

A mask was clamped on his face. All he could see was the white tile ceiling. His systolic pressure dropped by a half, but his heart continued to pump.

He needed blood and lots of it. He had lost almost half of the blood in his body, some 3500 cubic centimeters.

"Blood! Hurry!"

And new blood and strange blood was poured back into his body and with this spark of renewed life he spoke slowly, but clearly.

"I focused on that tiled ceiling and prayed. But I realized I couldn't ask for God's help while at the same time I felt hatred for the mixed up young man who had shot me. Isn't that the meaning of the lost sheep? We are all God's children and therefore equally beloved by him. I began to pray for his soul and that he would find his way back into the fold."

"I opened my eyes to find Nancy there. I pray I'll never face a day when she isn't there. In all the ways God has blessed me, giving her to me is the greatest and beyond anything I can ever hope to deserve."

And the world waited. He had been shot by a ".22 Devastator Bullet" designed to explode on impact.

MIRACULOUSLY the bullet did not explode on impact, but lodged deep in his chest just an inch from his heart.

IT WAS A MIRACLE HE HAD NOT BEEN KILLED!

Harry von Bulow

* * * * * *

Over two thousand years ago a young man named Stephen was killed by stoning by the religious leaders of his time. Stephen too, was trying to change the world, but when he denounced the Pharisees for murdering the Messiah, they killed him.

And then there was another one – Paul of Tarsus, who had led the mob at the stoning of Stephen. And later, on the Damascus Road, Paul was struck down and blinded by a light from heaven. And the Lord asked, "Paul, why do you persecute me?" And Paul was led back to Ananias and three days later his sight was restored. And Paul of Tarsus became Paul, the Apostle, one of the Lord's greatest, most brilliant evangelist.

On April 11th Reagan returned to the White House. He was still weak and in pain. He wrote: "I know it's going to be a long recovery. But whatever happens now, I owe my life to God and I will try to serve Him every way I can."

Thousands of letters, cards and even flowers flooded the White House: All of them praying for his recovery.

And he loved the ones that addressed him as "Dutch" for it brought back early memories, when he was a lifeguard, a sports announcer, a Midwestern kid, a college guy at Eureka; wonderful memories that brought a smile to his tired, pale face.

But there was one letter that caught his attention. It was addressed to "President Duch Reagan". Although "Dutch" was misspelled, it carried a poignant message from the past. It began:

"Dear Mr. President Duch Reagan,

GOD and Ronald Reagan
God moves in the affairs of men

I met you in the 20s in Lowell Park, Illinois. Do you remember the good times we had in the 20s. You were 17 years old then and everyone called you Duch. Please get well soon. We need you to save the country – remember all the lives you saved in Lowell Park."

The handwriting was shaky, possibly a touch of old age, but full of love by a woman who remembered that tall, good looking lifeguard at Lowell Park.

He loved it!

And then his old hometown, Dixon, Illinois sent him a picture of some hundred, or so people gathered under the famous Dixon Arch. And displayed in front of the hometown folks was a sign with giant letters spelling out their warm feelings for their local hero. It read:

"GET WELL DUTCH!"

Harry von Bulow

CHAPTER XIV

Reagan didn't get his inspiration for SDI from Star-Trek, or Star Wars. In 1967 as Governor of California, he visited the Lawrence Livermore laboratory in California, and talked with Edward Teller, the inventor of the hydrogen bomb. At that meeting Teller showed him some of the work that his students were doing on space-based lasers.

Teller was excited about them. "These lazers will soon be powerful and accurate enough that they could be used to destroy nuclear missiles fired at the U.S."

Reagan was impressed.

On July 31, 1979, Reagan visited the North American Air Defense Command (NORAD) buried deep in Cheyenne Mountains in Colorado. It was the control site for the launching of American nuclear weapons.

The commander of NORAD was Air Force General James Hill. "With our missile technology," he began, "we can hit targets in the Soviet Union with almost pinpoint precision."

GOD and Ronald Reagan
God moves in the affairs of men

"Terrific," replied Reagan. Then a moment later he asked the General, "What would happen if a Soviet missile was launched against the U.S.?" Reagan studied the General and then continued with the key question. "What could the U.S. do to prevent that?"

The General's reply was prompt. "Nothing," said General Hill. "We could do nothing."

"Nothing?" Reagan was shocked.

"Nothing," repeated Hill. "We can track the missile, but we can't knock it down."

"Does this mean that for all America spends annually on its defense budget, the nation is utterly defenseless against an enemy missile attack?"

General Hill nodded. "Yes."

In 1983 Reagan became convinced it was the right time for the U.S. to begin a program for missile defense. His decision was influenced by Admiral James Watkins, Chief of Naval Operations on the Joint Chief of Staff.

On March 23, 1985 Reagan gave an historic speech in which he asked American scientists to build a defense system against intercontinental missiles. Thus was born SDI, an ultimate weapon that would make intercontinental missiles obsolete!

Even his good friend George Schultz was skeptical of the idea. "We don't have the technology to do this."

Lawrence Eagleburger was shocked: "This changes the whole strategic doctrine of the U.S."

The defense department was opposed to it.

The cabinet, the agencies were shown copies of the speech. They refused to have anything to do with it. "It's not our idea. It's the president's idea; only his."

Adelman, head of the Arms Control and Disarmament Agency said, "It was made clear to me that the president liked the idea."

Harry von Bulow

The Soviet Union denounced the SDI proposal. Pravda said it was insane.

Robert McNamara termed it "pie in the sky."

Strobe Talbot of Time Magazine and later a member of the Clinton Administration stated: "It's more like an arcade video game."

The New York Times called it a "pipe dream, a projection of fantasy into policy."

The media named it "Star Wars" and roared with laughter. But the common guy on the street liked Star Wars and after all, in the picture, good conquers evil. What's wrong with that.

Ten months later the brilliant cynics began to modify their attack, when SDI brought Russia back to the bargaining table.

* * * * * *

Ten days after his inauguration the press met with Reagan.

"When are you going to propose a summit with the Soviets for arms control, Mr. President?"

"At present it's not a priority," said Reagan. There was a slight groan, which rumbled through the pressroom. And then Reagan continued, "Signed agreements mean nothing to the Soviets. The only morality they recognize is what will further their cause, meaning they reserve unto themselves the right to commit any crime, to lie, to cheat."

Another groan rumbled across the room. Even Secretary of State Alexander Haig glanced up at the ceiling and rolled his eyes. The reporter from Time opened his mouth in awe and didn't close it for five minutes.

* * * * * *

GOD and Ronald Reagan
God moves in the affairs of men

In Reagan's speech to the Evangelicals on March 9, 1983, he described the cold war as a "struggle between right and wrong, good and evil. He prophesized the demise of Russian communism and prayed for freedom throughout the world.

It was like ringing the Liberty Bell, heard 'round the world. It tolled for the oppressed, the downtrodden, and the enslaved.

Vaclav Hayel, President of Poland, called it a classic illustration of the "power of words to change history."

It began: "This Administration is motivated by a political philosophy that sees the greatness of America in you, her people, and in your families, churches, neighborhoods, communities – the institutions that foster and nourish values like concern for others and respect for the rules of law under God.

"Freedom prospers when religion is vibrant and the rule of law under God acknowledged. When our Founding Fathers passed the First Amendment, they sought to protect churches from government interference. They never meant to construct a wall of hostility between government and the concept of religious belief itself."

"The Declaration of Independence mentions the Supreme Being no less than four times; the Supreme Court opens its proceedings with a religious invocation; and the members of Congress open their sessions with a prayer. I just happen to believe the school children of the U.S. are entitled to the same privileges. Last year I sent the Congress a constitutional amendment to restore prayer to public schools.

"Let our children pray!"

Harry von Bulow

"I believe America is in the midst of a spiritual awakening and a moral renewal. With your Biblical keynote, I say today let 'justice roll on like a river, righteousness like a never failing-stream'."

"There is sin and evil in the world, and we are enjoined by Scripture and the Lord Jesus to oppose it with all our might. There is no room for racism, anti-Semitism, or other forms of ethic and racial hatred in this country. America has kept alight the torch of freedom – not just for ourselves, but for millions of others around the world. And this brings me to my final point today.

"During my first press conference as President, in answer to a direct question, I pointed out that as good Marxists-Leninists the Soviet leaders have openly and publicly declared that the only morality they recognize is that which will further their cause, which is world revolution. And their guiding spirit Lenin repudiated all morality that proceeds from supernatural ideas, or ideas that are outside class conceptions; morality being entirely subordinate to the interests of class war; and everything is moral that is necessary for the annihilation of the old exploiting social order and for uniting the proletariat.

"This does not mean we must isolate ourselves from them and refuse to seek an understanding with them, but at the same time, they must be made to understand we will never compromise our principles and standards. We will never give away our freedom. We will never abandon our belief in God."

"We will never stop searching for a genuine peace, but we feel that a freeze now of nuclear missiles would be a very dangerous fraud, an illusion of peace. The reality is that we must find peace through strength. I would agree to a freeze if only we could freeze the Soviets' global desires."

GOD and Ronald Reagan
God moves in the affairs of men

"Let us pray for the salvation of all those who live in totalitarian darkness; pray they will discover the joy of knowing God."

"But until they do, let us be aware that while they preach the supremacy of the state, declare its omnipotence over individual man, and predict its eventual domination of all people of the earth – they are the focus of EVIL in the modern world."

"It is a struggle between RIGHT AND WRONG, GOOD AND EVIL. While America's military strength is important, let me add here that I have always maintained that the struggle going on now for the world will never be decided by bombs, or rockets, by armies or military might. The real crisis we face today is a spiritual one; at root, it is a test of moral will and faith. I believe we shall rise to this challenge: I BELIEVE THAT COMMUNISM IS ANOTHER SAD, BIZZARRE CHAPTER IN HUMAN HISTORY WHOSE LAST PAGES EVEN NOW ARE BEING WRITTEN. I believe this because the source of our strength in the quest for human freedom is not material, but spiritual, and because it knows no limitation, it must terrify and ultimately triumph over those who would enslave their fellow man.

"For in the words of Isaiah: 'He giveth power to the faint; and to them that have no might He increaseth strength. But they that wait upon the Lord shall renew their strength; they shall mount up with wings as eagles; they shall run and not be weary.'"

But the next day the Washington Post condemned the president for his "good versus evil" approach.

The Times bellowed: "He'll take us to WWIII!"

The Post stormed: "Send him back to Hollywood before he sends us to hell!"

NBC quaked: "He doesn't know what he's doing."

Harry von Bulow

CBS reflected the same daunting fear: "He must retract that irresponsible statement: Retract! Retract Mr. President!" pleaded the CBS commentator.

Reagan retracted nothing!

* * * * * *

Late in '83 Reagan actually began negotiating with Russia, but strangely, all the Russian leaders were dying. He started with Brezhnev and he died. Then there was Andropov and he passed on. Next came Chernenko and he died. Nobody was killing them. They were dying quietly, serenely between the sheets in their own beds.

One Russian newsman blamed their demise on too much vodka.

Another said it was Stalin's ghost.

A Christian dissident, who was incarcerated in a gulag in Siberia said, "God is choosing."

"Choosing?" questioned his cellmate.

"Yes." And the Christian dissident rolled over on his iron cot and then murmured, "Praise the Lord."

"You're kidding," laughed another.

"There is no God," said the man with the gray speckled beard.

"He is here," said the Christian. "He is here. And he will pick the man."

"What's his name?"

"I don't know."

"I wish he would hurry."

GOD and Ronald Reagan
God moves in the affairs of men

CHAPTER XV

Nancy didn't want Ron to run for reelection in '84. She had had enough of Washington, D.C., its lying reporters, its liberal bias, and its bureaucratic confusion. She wanted to return to California and to a life of peace and quiet.

She was also concerned about his safety. She remembered the terrifying moment when he was shot by Hinckley. Only a miracle had saved his life, the bullet resting a millimeter from his heart. Then the riots at Berkeley, when student radicals tried to smash the windshield of the limo he was riding in. And the angry man in St. Louis waving a Colt .45 at him and it took two or three men to wrestle him to the ground (later it turned out to be a toy pistol, but no one knew at the time). And finally there was the constant angry, death-threatening calls that came in the dead of night; screaming voices crying for revenge. True, there hadn't been any actual attempts on his

Harry von Bulow

life recently, but as Nancy phrased it: "Why press your luck."

But Reagan hadn't finished the job. There were still some things to do. There was Russia and communism. It was still alive and growing: expanding into the Caribbean and southern Europe.

"I can't give in right now," he told Nancy. "We must finish the job."

And Nancy finally conceded. "If you feel that strongly about it, go ahead," she said, and then. "You know I'm not crazy about it, but okay."

Of course, the Times and the Post got it all wrong, their headlines blared: "NANCY INSISTS RON RUN!" And the story followed: Reagan wanted to retire, but his wife insisted that he run for a second term.

On January 29, 1984, in a broadcast from the Oval Office, Reagan announced his candidacy for a second term.

Nancy wrote in her diary: "I think it's going to be a tough, personal, close campaign. Mondale is supposed to be desperate. I'll be glad when the next nine months are over."

But the 1984 campaign turned out to be much easier than those in '76 and '80. There were two debates. Reagan always was a great debater, but surprisingly he lost the first match in Louisville. Kentucky to Mondale. The Reagan brain trust filled him with stacks of fact and turned the president into a CPA robot. This didn't work. Reagan was a leader, not a mechanical doll.

The Wall Street Journal headlines read: "IS THE OLDEST PRESIDENT NOW SHOWING HIS AGE?"

In the second debate, which was held in Kansas City, the old Reagan personality and humor returned. Henry Trewbitt of the Baltimore Sun asked about the so-called age factor.

GOD and Ronald Reagan
God moves in the affairs of men

Reagan's response: "I will not make this an issue in this campaign." Pause. Then, "I am not going to exploit, for political purposes, my opponent's youth and inexperience."

The audience laughed.

The old Reagan was back again! And he won the election by a landslide, winning every state except Minnesota and the District of Columbia.

But there were stormy times ahead: There was the Borg Affair, when an honorable man was smeared by a Democratic Congress: there was the Contra-Affair, when an omniscient Poindexter and Regan hid the critical information from the President. And then there was Nancy's cancer and thank God He spared her; and the Reykjavik Summit when Reagan thought he had reached an understanding with Russia, only to have it collapse at the last moment.

But the climax of his career, his life was still to come and it would happen in the final years of his presidency.

Harry von Bulow

CHAPTER XVI

On June 12, 1987 at 2:20 in the afternoon President Ronald Reagan made his famous, memorable speech, which rocketed around the world, including East Berlin which was still a Russian communist stronghold.

"Behind me stands a wall that encircles the free sector of this city, part of a vast system of barriers that divides the entire continent of Europe. From the Baltic, south, those barriers cut across Germany in a gash of barbed wire, concrete, dog runs, and guard towers. Farther south, there may be no visible, no obvious wall. But there remain armed guards and checkpoints all the same – still a restriction on the right to travel, still an instrument to impose upon ordinary men and women the will of a totalitarian state. Yet it is here in Berlin where the wall emerges most clearly; here, cutting across your city, where the news photo and the television screen have imprinted this brutal division of a continent upon the mind of the world. Standing before the Brandenburg Gate, every man is a

GOD and Ronald Reagan
God moves in the affairs of men

German, separated from his fellow men. Every man is a Berliner, forced to look upon a scar.

"In the 1950's, Khrushchev predicted: "We will bury you". But in the west today, we see a free world that has achieved a level of prosperity and well being unprecedented in all human history. In the Communist world, we see failure, technological backwardness; declining standards of health, even want of the most basic kind – too little food. Even today the Soviet Union still cannot feed itself. After four decades, then, there stands before the entire world one great and inescapable conclusion: Freedom leads to prosperity. Freedom replaces the ancient hatreds among the nations with comity and peace. Freedom is the victor.

"And now the Soviets themselves may, in a limited way, be coming to understand the importance of freedom. We hear much from Moscow about a new policy of reform and openness. Some political prisoners have been released. Certain foreign news broadcasts are no longer being jammed. Some economic enterprises have been permitted to operate with greater freedom from state control.

"Are these the beginnings of profound changes in the Soviet state? Or are they token gestures, intended to raise false hopes in the West, to strengthen the Soviet system without changing it? We welcome change and openness; for we believe that freedom and security go together, that the advance of human liberty can only strengthen the cause of freedom and peace.

"General Secretary Gorbachev, if you seek peace, if you seek prosperity for the Soviet Union and Eastern Europe, if you seek liberalization: come here to this gate, Mr. Gorbachev. Open this gate! Mr. Gorbachev, TEAR DOWN THIS WALL!"

And cheers of FREEDOM! FREEDOM! And shouts and cries of "Tear down this wall! Tear down this

Harry von Bulow

wall!" echoed through the streets of Berlin and around the world.

Although his mother Nelle had passed away over twenty years before, on this momentous occasion, she seemed almost in his presence. He could almost hear her voice repeating the story. She would always name the book, chapter and verse of the Bible. It's in Joshua Chapter 6, verse 16 to 20. And she would hold up her old, leather Bible and her voice would sing out as sweet and melodious as a turtle dove's.

Nancy studied his countenance. "Is there something wrong, dear?" she asked.

He shook his head, no. "Just thinking," he said. And in his mind the words of the story came back: *"And it came to pass at the seventh time, when the priests blew the trumpets, Joshua said unto the people, shout! For the Lord has given you the city. So the people shouted when the priests blew the trumpets; and the wall fell down flat, and the people went up into the city, and they took the city."*

"Ready to go, Ronnie?" asked Nancy.

"Yes, I'm ready now," he said. And he got into the limousine and as they drove away, he thought: I believe Nelle was with me today.

* * * * * *

Prayer was always a part of Ronald Wilson Reagan. From his childhood, to his youth and finally old age, prayer was the common denominator in his life. It brought him peace of mind even in the most difficult times. It isolated him from fear and gave him undaunting courage. And brought to him a solace that he found nowhere else.

As a young man, when he played football for Eureka College, he prayed before every game.

GOD and Ronald Reagan
God moves in the affairs of men

He prayed before critical conferences, critical world decisions. They were short, silent prayers, "Lord lead me. Guide me."

He prayed before the Gorbachev meeting.

He prayed as Governor of California, when he walked into a wild, raging mob at the University of California, where the students threw garbage at him; shouted angry epithets at him; and shoved dirty signs in his face and spit upon him. He needed a police escort to reach the main building, where he was going to make a speech. Even inside he felt their anger. They booed him, interrupted his speech, but Governor Reagan retained his poise.

He prayed when he fought the communists in Hollywood and when he appeared before the House Un-American Committee in Washington, D.C.

Like the courageous Cromwell, who feared no one, but God...

Like Martin Luther, who said, "One and God is a majority."

Reagan with God feared no one.

* * * * * *

On May 31, 1988 President Reagan arrived on the campus of Moscow State University. It was the alma mater of Mikhail Gorbachev and his wife Raisa. Reagan had wanted to meet and speak to the young people, the future of Russia, and Gorbachev consented to his request.

The auditorium at Moscow University was much larger than the one he remembered at Eureka College in DeKalb, Illinois, where he had graduated from many years before. The atmosphere was different too. There was little warmth in the room. In fact, it was cold and damp. More like a mausoleum than a college prep meeting. Hundreds of red flags hung from the ceiling. On its walls were paintings

Harry von Bulow

of its famous leaders: Joseph Stalin, Nikita Khrushchev and Breshnev. And then towering above the speaker's podium was a massive, white, marble bust of Lenin, its stone face silently surveying the entire proceedings.

Reagan knew he was in enemy country!

As he was introduced the auditorium grew silent; for a moment one could only hear the ticking of a large clock on distant wall. Then the university president clapped his hands; there followed an immediate response; applause echoed in the hall. It was almost robotical.

Reagan smiled. Looked into the eyes of the young men sitting before him. Then he began his speech; his soft, mellifluous voice floated serenely across the auditorium. There was a gentle touch of humor; a story about Bob Hope and John Wayne and even one of the Sundance Kid. Slowly and with dexterous care his voice melted into his major theme.

"Freedom," he said. "Human rights, God-given rights are the revolution of today. The Soviet Union cannot join in this revolution unless it allows greater freedom of thought, greater freedom of information, greater freedom of communication.

The president of the university coughed. He had something caught in his throat.

Reagan continued. "There is an air of change in the world today. And your country is an integral part of it." He paused and again studied the faces of the young people before him. "And only freedom can fulfill your dreams!"

Surprisingly there was a burst of applause as he ended his speech and a crowd of students came up, smiled and shook his hand and many asked for his autograph.

The czars of the Soviet news, however, were uncomfortable with Reagan. As a result, on their prime television news program "Vremya" they recorded only Reagan's official coming and going: getting in and out of

GOD and Ronald Reagan
God moves in the affairs of men

limousines, but almost nothing about the gist of his speech. To fill up the time they featured a sweet scene with Nancy Reagan visiting school No. 29; a toast at the Kremlin state dinner and an interview with Tom Brokaw of NBC.

President Reagan's remarks at Moscow State University were not reported. Nor did they appear in Izvestia the following day.

* * * * * *

But the voice of freedom, of human rights seems to generate its own momentum; like the "burning bush" it cannot be extinguished.

The next day Reagan visited the ancient Danilov Monastery, which recently had been returned to the Russian Orthodox Church. He gave a stirring sermon on religious freedom. It echoed throughout the ancient walls of the monastery. He called on the Soviet Union to reopen the thousands of boarded-up churches.

"End the oppression of banning religious groups."

The priests sat silent, awed by his bold remarks. It was words that hadn't been heard for years.

"Revoke the laws banning religious instruction!"

An under current of dismay and anxiety rippled through the ancient monastery.

Then he spoke of Solzenitzen, whose book on the Russian Gulags shook the world.

"Nobody speaks of Solzenitzen," murmured a bearded priest. "His name is poison here." He shook his head disconsolately. "Nobody," he repeated.

Then Reagan said, "Let us pray."

* * * * * *

Harry von Bulow

The next night Reagan hosted a highly publicized meeting with Christian dissidents. It was held at the U.S. Ambassador's residence.

It was a large gathering; many of the dissidents bringing their entire family. It was sort of a "once-in-a-lifetime event. Their years in the Soviet Union had been most difficult. They were the last to get employment; last to get a place to live (many families shared the same room). And last on the food chain. At least tonight they would get a good dinner (some even brought doggie bags). The parents and the children came scrubbed and clean. Some had patches on their pants, but they were neatly done. Some had problems with their shoes, some were a little too large and some featured paper in their soles. But they were God's people and Reagan treated them like kings and queens.

After they had filled their stomachs, the President stood up and made a toast. "I would like to make a toast to you, each of you, that stood boldly and courageously for God in a God-less country."

They cheered.

"The world is changing. Free people are gathering. So, take heart your day of freedom is coming soon."

They cheered.

"No longer will you have to hide. No longer will you have to run. No longer will you have to suffer."

And the cheers were louder and the applause longer.

And during the evening the President and Nancy listened to wild, tragic tales; and some with happy, glorious endings. But the stories that melted Reagan's heart most were the stories of the miracles that occurred to these people. They told of things that should never have happened. But did happen; of life-saving moments that were beyond comprehension.

GOD and Ronald Reagan
God moves in the affairs of men

And, as the gathering came to a close, Reagan led them in a prayer, praising the Lord and His goodness.

* * * * * *

Although the Russian news media – Esvestia and Tass, the official government agency, tried to ignore Reagan's voice of freedom it echoed like a drum-beat throughout Moscow and the Soviet Union.

And Gorbachev was cognizant of its beat!

* * * * * *

If Stalin, or Krushev had been head of the Soviet Union, it may have been more difficult for Reagan to free Russia from communism. Stalin had the heart of a gangster and he was only interested in personal power. He had become premier of Russia by literally killing all of his enemies – about thirty million. Machiavelli could have been his twin brother. And Krushev was made of the same material: In the U.S. he banged his shoes on a Congressional desk and swore, "We'll bury you!"

But Gorbachev was different. He had a grandmother who was a Christian. And, as a child, he probably sat on her lap as she told him stories about Christ and how he had given sight to the blind and cured the sick and made the cripples walk again. Gorbachev was acquainted with the Bible and Jesus. He probably was not a Christian, but he also was not a ruthless killer like Stalin. Gorbachev was an intelligent man, who thought more about his mother Russia than himself.

And Reagan felt he could trust him. They seemed to hit it off right from the start.

Nancy mentioned this to Gorbachev at a dinner in Moscow in May of 1988.

Harry von Bulow

During the dinner Gorbachev turned to Nancy and said, "You know, your husband and I have a certain…" he paused, searching for the right word.

"Let me help you," said Nancy. "Chemistry?"

"Yes, chemistry," he said.

"I know you do. I'm very aware of it, and so is my husband."

"It's very rare," said Gorbachev.

"I know that, too," said Nancy.

Then Gorbachev made a remarkable statement. "I am familiar with your Constitution, but I wish your husband could stay on for another four years."

Sometimes their conversations were light with a touch of humor. They told stories about themselves and their own country's bureaucratic foul-ups. They joked and laughed. Yes, believe it or not, Gorbachev laughed. A Russian leader laughed! That was a miracle in itself. Nor did Gorbachev have a calcified heart like Stalin. Two thousand years ago Stalin would have crucified Christ. Gorbachev would have listened like King Agrippa and almost be converted by Paul, the apostle.

Even Margaret Thatcher, Prime Minister of England, had a positive feeling about Gorbachev. She felt, like Reagan, that he could be trusted. She and Reagan had frequent discussions about the Russian leader and were convinced he was an honest man.

As a test Reagan asked Gorbachev to free some Christian dissidents that had been imprisoned by the Russian authorities. Reagan said he would certainly appreciate it and that he would not mention it to the press, nor anyone else. A few weeks later the Christians were released from prison.

It was true that Reagan's development of SDI, or Star Wars as the press described it, played a key role in influencing the Russian leaders; Gorbachev and certain

GOD and Ronald Reagan
God moves in the affairs of men

members of the politburo did believe that there was a possibility that something like SDI could be developed. But it was also obvious to them that it would cost billions of dollars and Russia did not have the money. In fact, at that time, the Soviet Union was suffering a major depression. They were having trouble even feeding their own people. Food was being rationed, gas was being rationed and there were millions of Russian people almost starving and freezing in the cold winter weather. Spending billions on an SDI type of program was impossible.

Russia's "evil empire" was about to expire. A new force, a democratic force, a force of freedom began to take shape. And Reagan was God's apostle. He was the Paul of the 20th Century. As Apostle Paul had had his Peter, Timothy and Luke; Reagan had his Thatcher and Hayel, President of Poland. And they turned the world upside down!

Harry von Bulow

CHAPTER XVII

On Friday, January 20, 1989 at 9:02 in the evening President Ronald Wilson Reagan made his Farewell Address.

"My fellow Americans: This is the 34th time I'll speak to you from the Oval Office and the last. We've been together eight years now, and soon it'll be time for me to go. But before I do, I wanted to share some thoughts. Some of which I've been saving for a long time.

"It's been the honor of my life to be your President. So many of you have written the past few weeks to say thanks, but I could say as much to you. Nancy and I are grateful for the opportunity you gave us to serve."

"One of the things about the Presidency is that you're always somewhat apart. You spent a lot of time going by too fast in a car someone else is driving, and seeing the people through tinted glass – the parents holding up a child, and the wave you saw too late and couldn't return. And so many times I wanted to stop and reach out

GOD and Ronald Reagan
God moves in the affairs of men

from behind the glass, and connect. Well, maybe I can do a little of that tonight.

"People ask how I feel about leaving. And the fact is, 'parting is such sweet sorrow.' The sweet part is California and the ranch and freedom. The sorrow – the goodbyes, of course, and leaving this beautiful place.

"You know, down the hall and up the stairs from this office is the part of the White House where the President and his family live. There are a few favorite windows I have up there that I like to stand and look out of early in the morning. The view is over the grounds here to the Washington Monument, and then the Mall and the Jefferson Memorial. But on mornings when the humidity is low, you can see past the Jefferson to the river, the Potomac, and the Virginia shore. Someone said that's the view Lincoln had when he saw the smoke rising from the Battle of Bull Run. I see more prosaic things: the grass on the banks, the morning traffic as people make their way to work, now and then a sailboat on the river.

"I've been thinking a bit at that window. I've been reflecting on what the past eight years have meant and mean. And the image that comes to mind like a refrain is a nautical one – a small story about a big ship, and a refugee and a sailor. It was back in the early eighties, at the height of the boat people. And the sailor was hard at work on the carrier Midway, which was patrolling the South China Sea. The sailor, like most American servicemen, was young, smart and fiercely observant. The crew spied on the horizon a leaky little boat. And crammed inside were refugees from Indochina hoping to get to America. The Midway sent a small launch to bring them to ship and safety. As the refugees made their way through choppy seas, one spied the sailor on deck and stood up, and called out to him. He yelled, 'Hello, American sailor. Hello, freedom man!'"

Harry von Bulow

A small moment with a big meaning, a moment the sailor, who wrote it in a letter, couldn't get it out of his mind. And, when I saw it, neither could I. Because that's what it was to be an American in the 1980's. We stood again for freedom. I know we always have, but in the past few years the world again – and in a way, we ourselves – rediscovered it.

"It's been quite a journey this decade, and we held together through some stormy seas. And at the end, together, we are reaching our destination."

"The fact is, from Grenada to the Washington and Moscow summits, from the recession of '81, or '82, to the expansion that began in late '82 and continued to this day, we've made a difference. The way I see it, there were two great triumphs, two things that I'm proudest of. One is the economic recovery, in which the people of America created – and filled – 19 million new jobs. The other is the recovery of our morale. America is respected again in the world and looked to for leadership.

"Something that happened to me a few years reflects some of this. It was back in 1981, and I was attending my first economic summit, which was held that year in Canada. The meeting place rotates among the member countries. The opening meeting was a formal dinner of the heads of government of the seven industrialized nations. Now, I sat there like a new kid in school and listened, and it was all Francois this and Helmut that. They dropped titles and spoke to one another on a first-name basis. Well, at one point I sort of leaned in and said, 'My name's Ron.' Well, in that same year, we began the actions we felt would ignite an economic comeback – cut taxes and regulation, started to cut spending. And soon the recovery began."

"Two years later, another economic summit with pretty much the same cast. At the big opening meeting we

GOD and Ronald Reagan
God moves in the affairs of men

all got together, and all of a sudden, just for a moment. I saw that everyone was just sitting there looking at me. And then one of them broke the silence. 'Tell us about the American miracle,'" he said.

"Well, back in 1980, when I was running for President, it was all so different. Some pundits said our programs would result in catastrophe. Our views on foreign affairs would cause war. Our plans for the economy would cause inflation to soar and bring about economic collapse. I even remember one highly respected economist say, back in 1982, that 'The engines of economic growth have shut down here, and they're likely to stay that way for years to come'. Well, he and the opinion leaders were wrong. The fact is what they call 'radical' was really 'right'. What they called 'dangerous' was just 'desperately needed.'"

"And in all of that time I won a nickname. 'The Great communicator.' But I never thought it was my style or words I used that made a difference; it was the content. I wasn't a great communicator, but I communicated great things and they didn't spring full bloom from my brow. They came from the heart of a great nation – from our experience, our wisdom, and our belief in the principles that have guided us for two centuries. They called it the Reagan revolution. Well, I'll accept that, but for me it always seemed more like the great rediscovery, a rediscovery of our values and our common sense."

"Common sense told us that when you put a big tax on something, the people will produce less of it. So, we cut the people's tax rates, and the people produced more than ever before. The economy bloomed like a plant that had been cut back and now grow quicker and stronger. Our economic program brought about the longest peacetime expansion in our history; real family income up, the poverty rate down, entrepreneurship booming, and an explosion in research and new technology. We're exporting more than

Harry von Bulow

ever because American industry became more competitive and at the same time, we summoned the national will to knock down protectionist walls abroad instead of erecting them at home.

"Common sense also told us that to preserve the peace, we'd have to become strong again after years of weakness and confusion. So, we rebuilt our defenses, and this New Year we toasted the new peacefulness around the globe. Not only have the superpowers actually begun to reduce their stockpiles of nuclear weapons – and hope for even more progress is bright – but the regional conflicts that rack the globe are also the beginning to cease. The Persian Gulf is no longer a war zone. The Soviets are leaving Afghanistan. The Vietnamese are preparing to pull out of Cambodia, and an American-mediated accord will soon send 50,000 Cuban troops home from Angola.

"The lesson of all this was, of course, that because we're a great nation, our challenges seem complex. It will always be this way. But as long as we remember our first principles and believe in ourselves, the future will always be ours. And something else we learned: Once you begin a great movement, there's no telling where it will end. We meant to change a nation, and instead, we changed a world."

"Countries across the globe are turning to free markets and free speech and turning away from the ideologies of the past. For them, the great rediscovery of the 1980's has been that, lo and behold, the moral way of government is the practical way of government: Democracy, the profoundly good, is also the profoundly productive."

"When you've got to the point when you can celebrate the anniversaries of your 39th birthday you can sit back sometimes, review your life, and see it flowing before you. For there was a fork in the river, and it was right in the

GOD and Ronald Reagan
God moves in the affairs of men

middle of my life. I never meant to go into politics. It wasn't my intention when I was young, but I was raised to believe you had to pay for the blessings bestowed on you. I was happy with my career in the entertainment world, but I ultimately went into politics because I wanted to protect something precious."

"Ours was the first revolution in the history of mankind that truly reversed the course of government, and with three little words: 'We the People.' We the people tell the government what to do; it doesn't tell us. 'We the People' are the driver; the government is the car. And we decide where it should go, and by what route, and how fast. Almost all the world's constitutions are documents in which governments tell the people what their privileges are. Our Constitution is a document in which 'We the People' tell the government what it is allowed to do. 'We the People' are free. This belief has been the underlying basis for everything I've tried to do these past 8 years.

"But back in the 1960's, when I began, it seemed to me that we'd begun reversing the order of things – that through more and more rules and regulations and confiscatory taxes, the government was taking more of our money, more of options, and more of our freedom. I went into politics in part, to put up my hand and say, 'Stop.' I was a citizen politician, and it seemed the right thing for a citizen to do."

"I think we have stopped a lot of what needed stopping. And I hope we have once again reminded people that man is not free unless government is limited. There's a clear cause and effect here that is as neat and predictable as a law of physics: As government expands, liberty contracts."

"Nothing is less free than pure communism – and yet we have, the past few years, forged a satisfying new closeness with the Soviet Union. I've been asked if this

Harry von Bulow

isn't a gamble, and my answer is no because we're basing our actions not on words but deeds. The détente of the 1970's was based not on action but promises. They'd promise to treat their own people and the people of the world better. But the gulag was still the gulag, and the state was still expansionist, and they still waged proxy wars in Africa, Asia and Latin America."

"Well, this time, so far, it's different. President Gorbachev has brought about some internal democratic reforms and begun the withdrawal from Afghanistan. He has also freed prisoners whose names I've given him every time we've met."

"But life has a way of reminding you of big things through small incidents. Once, during the heady days of the Moscow summit, Nancy decided to visit the shops on Arbat Street – that's a little street just off Moscow's main shopping area. Even though our visit was a surprise, every Russian there immediately recognized us and called out our names and reached for our hands. We were just about swept away by the warmth. You could almost feel the possibilities in all that joy. But within seconds, a KGB detail pushed their way toward us and began pushing and shoving the people in the crowd. It was an interesting moment. It reminded me that while the man on the street in the Soviet Union yearns for peace, the government is Communist. And those who run it are Communists, and that means we and they view such issues as freedom and human right very differently."

"We must keep up our guard, but we must also continue to work together to lessen and eliminate tension and mistrust. My view is that President Gorbachev is different from previous Soviet leaders. I think he knows some of the things wrong with his society and is trying to fix them. We wish him well. And we'll continue to work to make sure that Soviet Union that eventually emerges

GOD and Ronald Reagan
God moves in the affairs of men

from this process is less threatening one. What it all boils down to is this: I want the new closeness to continue. And it will, as long as we make it clear that we will continue to act in a certain way as long as they continue to act in a helpful manner. If and when they don't at first pull your punches. If they persist, pull the plug. It's still trust by verify. It's still play, but cut the cards. It's still watch closely. And don't be afraid to see what you see."

"I've been asked if I have any regrets. Well, I do. The deficit is one. I've been talking great deal about that lately, but tonight isn't for arguments, and I'm going to hold my tongue. But an observation: I've had my share of victories in the Congress, but what few people noticed is that I never won anything you didn't win for me. They never saw my troops, they never saw Reagan's regiments, the American people. You won every battle with every call you made and letter you wrote demanding action. Well, action is still needed. If we're to finish the job, Reagan's regiments will have to become the Bush brigades. Soon he'll be the chief, and he'll need you every bit as much as I did."

"Finally, there is a great tradition of warnings in Presidential farewells, and I've got one that's been on my mind for some time. But oddly enough it starts with one of the things I'm proudest of in the past 8 years; the resurgence of national pride that I called the new patriotism. This national feeling is good, but it won't count for much, and it won't last unless it's grounded in thoughtfulness and knowledge."

"An informed patriotism is what we want. And are we doing a good enough job teaching our children what America is and what she represents in the long history of the world? Those of us who are over 35 or 50 years of age grew up in a different America. We were taught, very directly, what it means to be an American. And we

Harry von Bulow

absorbed, almost in the air, a love of country and an appreciation of its institutions. If you didn't get these things from your family you got them from the neighborhood, from the father down the street who fought in Korea or the family who lost someone at Anzio. Or you could get a sense of patriotism from school. And if all else failed you could get a sense of patriotism from the popular culture. The movies celebrated democratic values and implicitly reinforced the idea that America was special. TV was like that, too, through the mid-sixties.

"But now, we're about to enter the nineties, and some things have changed. Younger parents aren't sure what an unambivalent appreciation of America is the right thing to teach modern children. And as for those who create the popular culture, well-grounded patriotism is no longer the style. Our spirit is back, but we haven't reinstitutionalized it. We've got to do a better job of getting across that American is freedom – freedom of speech, freedom of religion, freedom of enterprise. And freedom is special and rare. It's fragile; it needs protection."

"So, we've got to teach history based not on what's in fashion but what's important – why the Pilgrims came here, who Jimmy Doolittle was, and what those 30 seconds over Tokyo meant. You know 4 years ago on the 40th anniversary of D-day, I read a letter from a young woman writing to her late father, who'd fought on Omaha Beach. Her name was Lisa Zanatta Henn, and she said, 'we will always remember, we will never forget what the boys of Normandy did.' Well, let's help her keep her word. If we forget what we did, we won't know who we are. I'm warning of an eradication of the American memory that could result, ultimately in an erosion of the American spirit. Let's start with some basics: more attention to American history and a greater emphasis on civic ritual."

GOD and Ronald Reagan
God moves in the affairs of men

"And let me offer lesson number one about America: All great change in America begins at the dinner table. So, tomorrow night in the kitchen I hope the talking begins. And children, if your parents haven't been teaching you what it means to be an American, let 'em know and nail 'em on it. That would be a very American thing to do."

"And that's about all I have to say tonight, except for one thing. The past few days when I've been at that window upstairs, I've thought a bit of the 'shining city upon a hill'. The phrase comes from John Winthrop, who wrote it to describe the America he imaged. What he imagined was important because he was an early Pilgrim; an early freedom man. He journeyed here on what today we'd call a little wooden boat; and like the other Pilgrims, he was looking for a home that would be free. I've spoken of the shining city all my political life, but I don't know if I ever quite communicated what I saw when I said it. But in my mind it was a tall, proud city build on rocks stronger than oceans, windswept, God-blessed, and teeming with people of all kinds living in harmony and peace; a city with free ports that hummed with commerce and creativity. And if there had to be city walls, the walls had doors and doors were open to anyone with the will and heart to get here. That's how I saw it, and see it still."

"And how stands the city on this winter night? More prosperous, more secure, and happier than it was 8 years ago. But more than that: After 200 years, two centuries, she still stands strong and true on the granite ridge, and her glow has held steady no matter what the storm. And she's still a beacon, still a magnet for all who must have freedom, for all the pilgrims from all the lost places who are hurtling through the darkness, toward home."

"We've done our part. And as I walk off into the city streets, a final word to the men and women of the

Harry von Bulow

Reagan revolution, the men and women across America who for 8 years did the work that brought America back. My friends: We did it. We weren't just marking time. We made a difference. We made the city stronger, we made the city freer, and we left her in good hands. All in all, not bad, not bad at all."

"And so, goodbye. God bless you, and God bless the United States of America."

GOD and Ronald Reagan
God moves in the affairs of men

CHAPTER XVIII

When Reagan left office:

There was no inflation. The rate was 3%.

Interest rates had fallen to single digit.

Housing starts were up.

Gas prices had dropped. The oil crisis had ended.

Twenty million new jobs had been created between 1983 and 89.

The gross national product had increased by a third.

Harry von Bulow

Poverty and unemployment rates had declined.

The U.S. led the world in technology.

ABROAD HIS RECORD WAS EVEN MORE IMPRESSIVE:

When Reagan was elected democracy and capitalism were in retreat.

The USSR was the leader in the world.

Krushev boasted he would bury the U.S.

Most of the Third World countries were opting for some form of socialism, or Marxism.

In Latin America guerrilla revolutions were brewing, led by socialists, or communists.

The USSR, for the first time, surpassed the U.S. arsenal in nuclear weapons, including hundreds of long range SS-18 missiles. All targeted at the U.S.

Between 1974 and 1980 nine countries fell into the Soviet sphere: South Vietnam, Cambodia, Laos, South Ypemen, Angola, Mozambique, Ethiopia, Grenada and Nicaragua. Then the Soviets invaded Afghanistan.

GOD and Ronald Reagan
God moves in the affairs of men

DURING THE REAGAN ADMINISTRATION ALL THIS CHANGED.

Capitalism and democracy began to advance around the world:

Dictatorships collapsed in Chile, Haite and Panama.

Nine countries moved toward democracy:

Bolivia	1982
Honduras	1982
Argentina	1983
Grenada	1983
El Salvador	1984
Uruguay	1984
Brazil	1985
Guatemala	1985
Philippines	1985

Apartheid ended in South Africa.

ALL THESE CHANGES OCCURRED RELATIVELY PEACEFULLY.

In 1987 Russia agreed to dismantle and destroy its SS-20 missiles.

A year later it pulled its troops out of Afghanistan.

Harry von Bulow

Poland held it first free elections and Lech Walesa became president.

Suddenly all of Eastern and Central Europe was free!

AND THE BERLIN WALL CAME DOWN!

Boris Yeltsin became the first freely elected president of Russia.

So, in the twenty-first century, the United States found itself the world's sole super power and its political traditions of democracy and capitalism came to embody the aspirations of people everywhere in the world.

The century debate between capitalism and socialism was resolved.

This was no accident. Reagan was the prime mover. He was the architect of his own success.

He didn't do it alone. Margaret Thatcher, Pope John Paul II, Vuclav Havel and Lech Walesa helped.

BUT REAGAN WAS THE DECISIIVE AGENT OF CHANGE!

Reagan was the visionary. He saw the world through the clear lens of right and wrong.

And this clear perception of right and wrong, justice and injustice came from the teachings of his mother Nelle, who nightly read to him and his brother the Scriptures. The Bible teaches that good will eventually overcome evil. And Reagan believed this implicitly.

There was a Christian root to almost every belief that Reagan held. And these beliefs were never compromised. No political faction, no pompous professor,

GOD and Ronald Reagan
God moves in the affairs of men

nor intellectual wiseacre ever changed, nor compromised these beliefs. Reagan had become God's modern day apostle, an apostle of hope and trust. He also had a certain providential understanding of his destiny and that of his country. In this respect he was much like Abraham Lincoln, who constantly read the Bible.

Great leaders view the entire landscape and detect which issues are absolutely decisive. Like Lincoln Reagan had the unerring capacity to separate things that mattered from things that did not. Both seemed to approach difficult situations with unusual confidence and then solved them with almost child-like simplicity.

Reagan didn't care about power for its own sake, but he was ambitious mainly for the triumph of his ideas. Unlike many who seek office, he wanted to be president for one reason only: To realize his principles and improve his country and the world.

And he was most tenacious about his moral and political beliefs. No matter what anybody said he would not give in. He was unique among politicians: He was incorruptible and cared nothing for personal glory. The sign in his office read: "There is no limit to what a man can do, or where he can go if he doesn't mind who gets the credit."

And when it came to a point of principle he was impervious to personal attacks. Speech writers came and left, yet Reagan's message remained the same. As Reagan put it, "We meant to change a nation and instead we changed the world."

The wise men of the world. The intellectual snobs, most of the diehard liberals and even some of his own party members made fun of him and scorned him.

Two thousand years ago Jesus suffered the same contempt. His hometown of Nazareth never accepted him as the Messiah.

Harry von Bulow

"Isn't this the carpenter's son?" asked the Sadducees. They were the rich and famous, the liberals in Jesus' time.

And the Pharisees questioned his validity too. "What good ever came out of Nazareth?" they asked.

And the Sadducees never accepted the miracles that Jesus performed. When they were told that he had walked on the water one stormy night on the Sea of Galilee, they laughed and said, "HE must have been near the shore and was walking on the sand."

And the proud religious leaders, the Pharisees feeling their power being usurped by Jesus accused Him of being Beezlebub, the devil.

* * * * * *

Today in this sophisticated, cynical world people rarely believe in miracles. They seem outside our realm of perception. Miracles only happened two thousand years ago during the time of Christ. But not in our time!

But let us pause and reflect:

President John Kennedy couldn't free the tiny island of Cuba from its dictator Castro. Thousands of anti-communist, anti-Castro fighters died on the beaches of Cuba.

President Carter could not free the hostages in Iran. And eight men died in the desert sand.

Eisenhower, along with the allies, DID free Europe from Hitler in WWII, but millions of young men lost their lives.

President Lincoln freed the slaves in one of the bloodiest wars our country has ever fought: the Civil War.

President Ronald Reagan freed millions of Russian people from communism and slavery...

Without Firing a Shot.

GOD and Ronald Reagan
God moves in the affairs of men

THAT'S A MIRACLE!!

Only with God's help could such a miracle take place.

Harry von Bulow

GOD and Ronald Reagan
God moves in the affairs of men

POSTSCRIPT

And like Paul, the Apostle who suffered from a wound that would never heal, Ronald Wilson Reagan, a true man of God, suffers with Alzheimer's, which destroys the memory of things past.

Today he lives in a no-man's land sharing dreams with his lovable, faithful Nancy; living at Rancho de Cielo, a ranch in the clouds; his past lost in the sunlight and shadows of the world he loved.

It is one of the mysteries of all mysteries: why men who loved God suffer so much. The Lord must have a special place for them. Amen.

Harry von Bulow

GOD and Ronald Reagan
God moves in the affairs of men

BIBLIOGRAPHY

"BIBLE" King James Version

Edmund Morris: "Dutch" (New York 1999)

Reagan, Maureen. "First Father, First Daughter" (Boston 1989)

Reagan, Michael, "On the Outsdie Looking in" (New York 1988)

Reagan, Ronald with R.G. Hublr: "Where's the Rest of Me?" Autobiography of Ronald Reagan.

Reagan, Nancy with William Novak: "Memoires of Nancy Reagan."

Regan: "For the Record."

D'souza, Dinesh: "Ronald Reagan" (New York 1997)

Davis, Patti: "The Way I See It" (New York 1992)

Hannaford, Peter.: The Reagans. "A Political Portrait."

Will, George, "How Reagan Changed America." (Newsweek Jan. 1989)

Brown, Edmund "Pat" and Bill Brown." Reagan: The Political Chameleon." (New York 1976)

Shultz, George: "Turmoil and Triumph! My Years as Secretary of State." (New York 1993)

Harry von Bulow

ABOUT THE AUTHOR

Von Bulow is a world traveler, writer and broadcaster.

Has sampan'd in China, raced up the klongs in those pencil-thin, high powered canoes in Borneo, swam with stingrays off Jamaica; trudged up the Delarosa in Jerusalem, and climbed down into the pharaoh's tombs in Egypt.

He has written for newspapers (Star and Plain Talk) and radio and television. His first book was an autobiography "From Here to Eternity Without a Road Map"; then a political book, "The President's Wife", followed by "My Father, the President"; all are a part of political triology. Other books by the author are: "They Called Him Meshuga, Crazy Man", the story of Noah and the great flood. And his last book is a love story, a true story entitled: "The Travels of Jerry Smith and Raggedy Ann", and finally a biography of his favorite President: Ronald Wilson Reagan.

Von Bulow enjoys golf, tennis and swimming. Has four children and fourteen grandchildren. He writes and lives in Southern California.

Printed in Great Britain
by Amazon